THE
PAN-AFRICAN LOVE STORY
of
ARNOLD and MIGNON FORD

The Story of a Pan African Journey from Barbados to Ethiopia,
From the Marcus Garvey Movement to the
Nation Building Mission of Emperor Haile Selassie

DAVID COMISSIONG

October, 2020.

David Comissiong Publishing
Clement Payne Cultural Centre
Crumpton Street, Bridgetown, Barbados

ISBN (paperback): 978-976-96537-0-2

This book is dedicated to

*the memory of **Professors Cecil Crawford** and **Abiyi Ford**,*

both of whom committed themselves to honouring the legacies of

***Arnold Josiah Ford** and **Mignon Lorraine Inniss Ford**,*

and to telling the story of their inspirational lives.

Table of Contents

Introduction

David Comissiong

The **Pan-African Love Story of Arnold and Mignon Ford** is a book that I felt that I was duty bound to write.

From the very first time that I was exposed to the life stories of Arnold Josiah Ford and Mignon Lorraine Inniss Ford – way back in the late 1980s – I felt a spiritual connection to these two outstanding Pan-Africanists and thenceforth made it my business to verbally spread the stories of their remarkable lives and contributions.

Indeed, whenever we sang the **Universal Ethiopian Anthem** at Pan-Africanist events, I made it a point of duty to enlighten the audience about the Barbadian origin of the composer of this legendary black anthem – Arnold Josiah Ford. And then, sometime in the late 1990s, I had the good fortune to meet and befriend Professor Abiyi Ford, the younger son of Arnold and Mignon.

Indeed, in my capacity as Director of the Barbados government's **Commission for Pan-African Affairs** I was able to play host to Abiyi in Barbados, and to help to organize a number of his public engagements. And it was this relationship with Abiyi that facilitated my acquisition of additional biographical information about Abiyi's illustrious parents.

Needless to say, I am convinced that Arnold Josiah Ford and his wife, Mignon Lorraine Inniss Ford, are two of the greatest Barbadians of all times, and that their heroic life stories are required reading for all Barbadian and other Caribbean people – indeed for all black or African people!

Arnold and Mignon Ford are valuable role models for our people, particularly our youth. Here, revealed before our eyes, are two extremely conscious and committed Barbadians – conscious of their African-ness, of their glorious heritage and of the heroic struggles of their forefathers, and absolutely committed to the advancement of their people – **all** of their people – in Africa and throughout the African Diaspora.

Furthermore, these two biographies have the added value of bringing us into close and intimate contact with some of the most compelling and important episodes and developments in the 20th century history of Africa and the African Diaspora. Thus, as you read this book, you will come into contact not only with the thrilling and inspirational personal life stories of Arnold and Mignon, but also with:-

- the pioneer African-American musician, James Reese Europe, and the early development of the classical music of Black America;
- the Right Excellent Marcus Mosiah Garvey and his **Universal Negro Improvement Association** (UNIA);
- the history of Ethiopia, from ancient times to the 20th century;
- the story of the composition of the Marcus Garvey version of the Universal Ethiopian Anthem;
- the Black Jewish movement of the United States of America;
- the Coronation of Emperor Haile Selassie I;
- the story of the composition of the Rastafarian version of the Universal Ethiopian Anthem;
- the Italian invasion and occupation of Ethiopia;
- the story of the legendary **Princess Zennebe Worq School** of Ethiopia; and
- the story of the overthrow of Emperor Haile Selassie I .

The **Pan-African Love Story of Arnold and Mignon Ford** is therefore choc-a-bloc with historical information that is critical for the process of fostering progressive black consciousness and facilitating the development of a strong and empowering sense of black or African identity.

For well over twenty years, I knew that I **had** to write this book, but it wasn't until the COVID-19 based "lockdown" of March to May 2020 that I actually found the time to sit down and put pen to paper. This book is therefore, at least, one positive outcome of the COVID-19 pandemic!

I consider this book to be a mere introduction to the life stories of these two towering black heroes, and it is my hope that my modest effort will encourage our professional historians to produce much more comprehensive and definitive biographies.

DAVID COMISSIONG
Barbados' Ambassador to
the Caribbean Community (CARICOM)

Foreword

Dr. Myrna Belgrave

*"Ethiopia thou land of our fathers,
Thou land where the gods loved to be"*

These beginning lines of the **Universal Ethiopian Anthem** are sung by Pan-Africanists around the world as they affirm the love which they hold in their hearts for the country of Ethiopia.

I once did a study tour of Ethiopia and returned with many memorable and elevated insights into the spirit of African humanity. It was, to say the least, an informative, captivating and exhilarating visit, full of highlights.

Take for example, the airline flight from **Addis Ababa** - the capital of Ethiopia - to the holy city of **Lalibela**. This experience revealed a natural terrain that was overwhelming in its beautiful scenic shapes and forms. The mountains were stately and seemed to be carved with the exactness, infinite mystery and wisdom of the Divine, truly creating a space where the "gods loved to be".

My experience during that visit was simply one of wonder and ancestral pride!

Another example is the architecture of the distinctive subterranean churches carved out of rocks in Lalibela. These structures reveal the innate self- worthiness, creativity and inspired knowing of the people of this ancient land. There are wall hangings that depict images of the black Madonna and Child surrounded by black choir boys with upturned cherub collars—an image that, I am told, inspired the fashion template of choir boys in western cathedrals.

And peace is the feeling that emerges when visiting **Aksum**, the centre of ancient Africa, with its famous obelisk. The centuries-old **St. Mary of Zion Sanctuary** houses the biblical Ark of the Covenant and reflects again a religious self-worthiness, a mystical and quiet admiration for ancestral history.

Ethiopia, on many levels, is a citadel of ancient African awareness, courage and resilience - a country that has never been conquered by outsiders. And it is in this mystical ancient setting that our Pan-Africanist, Barbados-born hero and heroine, **Rabbi Arnold Josiah Ford** and **Mignon Lorraine Inniss Ford**, chose to consummate their love affair both for their ancestry and for each other.

Their personal contributions to Ethiopia in music and education are very well detailed in this book entitled **The Pan-African Love Story of Arnold and Mignon Ford**. Indeed, it is a love story that began long before they set foot on the sacred soil of Ethiopia - back in the days when they were both members of the **Marcus Garvey** movement in the United States of America. This Pan-African love story is therefore also a story of Marcus Garvey and his **Universal Negro Improvement Association (UNIA)**.

I had the distinct pleasure of meeting and interacting with a son of this distinguished Pan-African union - the late **Abraham (Abiyi) Ford**- and with Abiyi's daughter, **Miniabiyi**.

Abiyi was an embodiment of the biography that I had read about him - *"Spiritually, intellectually and creatively, Abraham (Abiyi) Ford, was a man of many worlds."* Indeed, he *"seamlessly embodied his varied Ethiopian and Caribbean cultural identities, honouring and celebrating both with his personal and professional contributions."*

During my visit to Ethiopia, Abiyi showed me his mother's school - a school which now stands in ruins, but which carries a rich history of the contribution made by Mignon Lorraine Inniss Ford to the nation of Ethiopia.

Abiyi was one of a few young boys enrolled in the **Princess Zenebe Worq School,** and it was here that Abiyi learned the values of service and community that became the guiding tenets of his life.

Abiyi narrated and guided me through the ruins of the school, explaining and reliving the history of each room. His pride was evident. As an educator myself who had spent five years training teachers in Nigeria, I felt a deep connection with Mignon's pioneering adventurous spirit and her love for ancestry. That love drew her to share her skills and her life with her ancestral roots.

Standing there amid the ruins, my Bajan pride was ignited. The magic and mystique of the land, together with the visible evidence of the contributions made by my fellow Barbadians, just flooded my being with happiness and has left an invaluable imprint even as I recall and write this memory.

Years later I met Abiyi in Washington D.C., still sharing and basking in the pride generated by the contributions of his parents to Ethiopia. It was at this time that he initiated the **Mignon Ford Foundation**, with the aim of creating a documentary of the school and starting a rebuilding process.

An outreach arm of the Foundation was started in Barbados, and the late **Cecil Crawford** and I became the trustees of that Barbadian branch. It was an honour for both of us.

The concept of Pan-Africanism emerged from the hearts of those who love their African roots and who understood their worthiness on many levels. It is a call to reclaim the greatness of these roots. It offers a far-sighted and important vision of past, present and future, and instils a purpose that makes our living ever meaningful, even with its difficult moments.

And in our long historical journey we discover many exciting historical contributions that are worthy of being captured for posterity. They are the stuff that creates stories of interest like **The Pan-African Love Story of Arnold and Mignon Ford**. I therefore invite you to read, learn, honour and enjoy the journey of these two illustrious ancestors - **Arnold Josiah Ford** and **Mignon Lorraine Inniss Ford**.

The story of their lives and of their love for Africa has been well researched and written by the author, **Ambassador David Comissiong**. I commend it to you as an important contribution to the on-going mission of rediscovering our glorious African heritage.

DR. MYRNA BELGRAVE

THE
PAN-AFRICAN LOVE STORY
of
ARNOLD and MIGNON FORD
(Part 1)

ARNOLD'S STORY

"Princes shall come out of Egypt and Ethiopia shall soon stretch forth her hands unto God." (Psalm 68, Verse 31)

Chapter 1

A Legend Is Born

OUR STORY begins with a scene in a room in a small house in Addis Ababa, the capital city of the African kingdom of Ethiopia. It is September 1935, and lying on his death-bed in the room is a fifty-eight year old black Barbadian man by the name of **Arnold Josiah Ford**. Also in that room is Arnold's much younger Barbadian wife – **Mignon Inniss Ford** – and their two newly born Ethiopian children, Yosif and Abiyi.

Arnold Josiah Ford is the most important leader of the West Indian and African-American community in Ethiopia – in fact he is the leader of a project to establish an agricultural settlement of repatriated "Black Jews" of the Diaspora on several hundred acres of land provided by Emperor Haile Selassie. But as a result of extreme stress and overwork to the point of the destruction of his health, Arnold's life is slipping away, and the last mission he seeks to perform is to extract from his young wife a solemn pledge that, come what may, she would never leave or abandon Ethiopia.

Fascist Dictator, Benito Mussolini

You see, in September 1935, Ethiopia – the one African kingdom that had never been conquered or colonized – was facing a moment of extreme existential crisis! The brutal fascist Italian dictator, Benito Mussolini, had made clear his evil intention to invade, conquer and colonize Ethiopia, and had started the process by amassing a formidable array of military forces in the territories bordering Ethiopia.

And so, what promised to be a genocidal military invasion was imminent, leading most of the fearful African-American and Caribbean migrants in Ethiopia to flee the country in haste.

But who exactly - you may ask – was this dutiful, Ethiopia-loving Bajan man, and what had led him to journey so many thousands of miles from his Caribbean island home to meet his maker in this legendary ancient African kingdom?

Well, let us wend our way back to Arnold's Barbadian island home and start at the very beginning.

Arnold Josiah Ford was born in Bridgetown, Barbados at exactly 5:30 PM on the 23rd day of April 1877 – a mere thirty-nine years after the abolition of Slavery, and one year after the "Confederation Rebellion" in which virtually starving, land hungry black Barbadians had unsuccessfully taken up arms against the white plantocracy that ruled the British colony.

Plantation Labourers in 19th Century Barbados

Late 19th Century, Bridgetown, Barbados

Arnold's father was Edward Ford - a policeman who also served as a "fiery" Local Preacher in the Methodist Church - and his mother was Elizabeth Augusta Brathwaite. The family is reputed to have resided in the eastern parish of St. Joseph, on the Atlantic coast side of the island of Barbados, some 2,900 miles across the ocean from the west coast of Africa. As an adult, Arnold Josiah Ford would always insist that his father's ancestry could be traced back to the Yoruba tribe of Nigeria, and that his mother's ancestry was rooted in the Mendi tribe of present day Sierra Leone.

In addition, the Ford family lore maintained that their heritage extended even further back to one of the priestly families of the ancient (black) Israelites. Indeed, even though Arnold was baptized in the Methodist Church and would have officially been a Methodist, his family maintained customs and traditions that identified them with Judaism.

But what is extremely significant about Arnold's late 19th century childhood in racist, colonial Barbados is that his parents were so determined that he should become an accomplished musician, that they provided him with private tutors who instructed him in several instruments – particularly the harp, violin and bass. And it soon became clear that Arnold had no ordinary talent for music! Indeed, it would not be an exaggeration to say that the multi instrument Barbadian musician was something of a musical prodigy.

Eventually, in 1899 - at the age of 22 years - the talented young Barbadian musician joined the British Royal Navy; was assigned to the Navy's musical corps; and served as a "master musician" for several years on the military ship HMS Alert. He travelled to many parts of the world, including – very significantly – the continent of Africa.

It is not known exactly how many years young Arnold served in the British Navy, but we do know that sometime during the latter part of the first decade of the 20th century he was resident in Bermuda and served as a clerk of the Court of Federal Assize in that British colony. Ford also claimed to have lived and worked in the West African Republic of Liberia for some period of time during that decade. And we can also place the peripatetic Barbadian in the City of London between 1909 and 1910, where he took lessons in musical theory with that distinguished black Jamaican, the Honourable Edmonstone Barnes.

The year of 1910 was a "Year of Destiny" for the then thirty-three year old Barbadian, for this was the year in which he migrated to the then mecca of the Black World – Harlem in New York City – and commenced the most fertile and creative period of his life.

The Young Arnold Ford

Arnold would not have been aware of it then, but he was migrating to Harlem at the very start of that remarkable era of intellectual, social and artistic flowering that came to be known as the **New Negro Movement** or the **Harlem Renaissance.**

Indeed, the era was so fertile for Arnold Josiah Ford – in so many ways – that sometime during his early years in Harlem he became intimately involved with and married a woman by the name of Olive Nurse. Unfortunately, we know little or nothing about Olive Nurse, although if we were to speculate, we would be tempted to claim her as a Barbadian, since the name Olive Nurse is such a Barbadian name! What we do know however, is that the marriage is said to have produced two children, and to have lasted until 1924, when - unfortunately - it ended in divorce.

But let us set the stage for an exploration of the "Harlem Years" by describing some critical elements of the Harlem that Arnold migrated to, particularly in relation to music – African American music.

Chapter 2

Making It In Harlem

In 1904 - six years before Arnold Josiah Ford's arrival in Harlem - the famous African-American musician, **James Reese Europe**, had responded to the predicament of black New York City musicians who were finding it extremely difficult to ply their trade as professional musicians, by establishing an institution known as the **New Amsterdam Musical Association** (NAMA) - a trade union specifically for black musicians.

James Reese Europe

You see, in that era, the laws of New York stipulated that a musician was only entitled to work in the City if he or she was a member of a trade union, and the only musicians' unions in New York city were "whites only" unions! Thus, the establishment of the NAMA in 1904 was a critical event in the development of Black Music, and as we shall see, it was an institution that came to play a big role in the life of the Barbadian musical genius, Arnold Josiah Ford.

Furthermore, as an adjunct to the NAMA, James Reese Europe went on in 1910 to establish the **Clef Club** – a popular black entertainment venue and "society", and the home base of Europe's mind-blowing and precedent-setting one hundred and twenty-five member strong black orchestra. The Clef Club quickly became a nesting place and an incubator of outstanding black musical talent. For example, in the early days, its membership included such innovators as Willie "The Lion" Smith, master of the stride piano.

It was these two institutions – the NAMA and the Clef Club – that, along with the **Hebrew religion**, came to form the centre of gravity of Arnold Josiah Ford's life during his early years in Harlem. Indeed, in these early Harlem days it was all about music and religion for the driven and ambitious multi-talented Barbadian!

Black Musicians organized by James Europe

Now, we have already recorded that the Ford family-lore contained the notion that the family was ultimately descended from an ancient priestly Israelite clan, and that Jewish practices were part of the family culture. While living in Harlem, the Barbadian encountered a group calling themselves "Ethiopian Hebrews" – black Jews – who maintained that Blacks were derived from one of the lost tribes of Israel, and who identified this "lost tribe" with the Falashas, a people living in Ethiopia and practising a simplified form of Judaism. Ford was fascinated by this sect and commenced study of the Torah, Talmudic Law, and the Hebrew Language.

Arnold Josiah Ford reasoned that if so many of the ancient Hebrews were black, then Judaism had to be as much a part of the African's cultural and religious heritage as Christianity. So, not only did he self-identify as a Black Jew, but in addition to studying the Hebrew religion and language, he ultimately secured ordination as a Rabbi. Indeed, he was well known in Harlem circles as Rabbi Arnold J Ford.

It also needs to be noted that the Barbadian possessed a general interest in mysticism, esoteric knowledge, and secret societies, and that this manifested itself in his membership in the **Scottish Rite Masons**, where he served as Master of the Memmon Lodge for a few years.

And so far as the music was concerned - in 1912 the Barbadian master musician achieved the distinction of being installed as the Director and Band Master of the NAMA, a position that he held up until the year 1920. In addition, and equally as important, he also became a member of James Reese Europe's famous and historic **Clef Club Orchestra**.

The Clef Club Orchestra

Now, in order to appreciate the massive historical significance of these two developments, one needs to be aware of some seminal elements in the history of Black Music.

One needs to be aware, for example, that James Reese Europe and the Clef Club Orchestra played a critical role in the development of the classical music of Black America, by inter alia: championing the playing of orchestral music written by black composers such as **Samuel Coleridge–Taylor** and **Harry T. Burleigh**; popularizing the urban, North-Eastern USA "Ragtime" music of the African American community; pioneering the development of **Jazz** music with their original proto-Jazz compositions; leading the way for Black Music with a series of historic phonograph recordings for the **Victor Talking Machine Company**; and by taking Black Music to dizzying heights with a series of critically acclaimed concerts at the prestigious **Carnegie Hall** between 1912 and 1915.

I would like to stress that the Clef Club Orchestra was a massive orchestra of some one hundred and twenty-five members, and that it performed on various occasions at the prestigious Carnegie Hall. In order to get a sense of what this historic orchestra represented, it is instructive to read a comment from a music review in the **New York Times** of March 12, 1914: *"...the programme consisted largely of plantation melodies and Spirituals....arranged such as to show that.....these composers are beginning to develop an art of their own based on their folk material"*.

Indeed, when James Reese Europe and his ground-breaking Clef Club Orchestra were criticized by Euro-centric music critics, this is how Europe responded and explained the significance of the work that men like himself and Ford were accomplishing:-

"We have developed a kind of symphony music that, no matter what else you think, is different and distinctive, and that lends itself to the playing of the peculiar compositions of our race ..... My success has come .... from a realization of the advantages of sticking to the music of my own people .... We coloured people have our own music that is part of us ... It is the product of our souls; it's been created by the sufferings and miseries of our race".

This was the early development and coming of age of the African-American's classical music - Spirituals and Jazz. And, needless to say, the presence and input of our Barbadian musical hero – Arnold Josiah Ford – is to be found in these historic developments. In light of this, the Barbadian musician

– Arnold Josiah Ford – has to be considered one of the legends and heroes of Black Music and one of the architects of the Harlem Renaissance!

Master Musician Arnold Ford In Harlem

Chapter 3

Joining the Marcus Garvey Movement

By now it should have become clear that we have embarked upon the mission of telling the life story of a very outstanding black hero: a pioneer who - from very early in his career - consciously saw himself as a black nationalist leader engaged in the task of building a new black aesthetic, a new black community, a new black nation, a new black Civilization!

Thus, it would have surprised no-one when, in or about the year 1917, Rabbi Ford – a well-known and highly respected Rabbi of the black Hebrew faith - threw in his lot with the then emerging black nationalist leader, **Marcus Mosiah Garvey**, and became a member of the Harlem branch of Garvey's **Universal Negro Improvement Association** (UNIA) .

Marcus Mosiah Garvey

No doubt, Rabbi Ford would have seen in Marcus Garvey a kindred spirit – a fellow West Indian who had migrated to Harlem from the Caribbean island of Jamaica for the express purpose of developing a mass organization devoted to uplifting the entire black or African race, instilling racial pride in black people, and generating independent black economic enterprise. The vehicle that Garvey established in Kingston, Jamaica in 1914 to carry out this massive and historic mission was the **Universal Negro Improvement Association and African Communities League** commonly abbreviated as **UNIA**.

In 1916, Garvey - President of the UNIA - migrated to the United States of America; undertook a highly successful thirty-eight State speaking tour of the USA; and launched a New York branch of the UNIA in May 1917. It was this Harlem-based branch of the UNIA that the Barbadian musician felt moved to join and to contribute to.

The circumstances surrounding the Barbadian musician cum Rabbi linking up with the great Marcus Garvey are as follows: this was the period of the First World War, and the year of 1917 saw James Reese Europe taking temporary leave from NAMA and the Clef Club, enlisting in the all-black **369th United States Infantry Regiment** (the so-called "Harlem Hellfighters"), and making his way to France where he distinguished himself not only as a soldier, but also as the leader of the all black Regimental musical band playing "black" or "Negro" music. But Ford, who was by then a highly regarded black Jewish religious leader and musician, opted to remain in Harlem.

James Reese Europe conducting his Military Band

It was in these circumstances that the Barbadian took up duties as the Musical Director of the UNIA choir.

Also of significance is that Ford took with him to the UNIA choir such fellow black Jews as **Samuel Valentine** (President of the choir) and **Nancy Paris** (lead singer). Indeed, Ford and these two talented singers went on to form the core of an active group of black Jews within the UNIA. And not only did they study the Hebrew language, religion and history, but they also held Jewish religious services at "Liberty Hall", the headquarters of the UNIA.

Ford initially tried to prevail upon Marcus Garvey to adopt Judaism as the official religion of the UNIA, but although Garvey rejected this idea, Rabbi Ford still agreed to place his musical skills at the service of the UNIA. And, needless to say, Rabbi Ford did go on to make the Black-Jewish dynamic an important component of the UNIA.

As a paid UNIA officer, Rabbi Ford was responsible for orchestrating much of the amazing pageantry of the UNIA's highly attractive ceremonies. He served as director of the UNIA's band and orchestra, and as leader of the band of the para military arm of the UNIA – the **African Legion** – which regularly paraded through the streets at the head of UNIA processions. As noted before, he was also musical director of the Choir at Liberty Hall, the UNIA's national headquarters in Harlem, and he wrote dozens of UNIA songs, many of which were published in the **Universal Ethiopian Hymnal**.

In addition, Ford quickly distinguished himself by composing a brilliant musical anthem that was initially titled **"Ethiopia"**, and that immediately caught the attention of Garvey and the top leadership of the UNIA. (But to be absolutely correct, we should note that while Ford alone composed the music, he collaborated with one Benjamin Burrell in composing the lyrics.)

It seems clear that the lyrics of the song had been inspired by the famous biblical verse found in Psalm 68 - ***"Princes shall come out of Egypt and Ethiopia shall soon stretch forth her hands unto God"***. This was a Bible verse that had resonated among the enslaved African people of the Caribbean and Americas from since the dark and dismal years of Slavery, and had long inspired hope in a coming era of African Redemption.

The term ***"Ethiopia"*** - the title of the song - had long been regarded as a name for the entire continent of Africa. However, when - in 1896 - Blacks in the Americas heard the startling news about an actual independent African kingdom in North-East Africa, by the name of **Ethiopia**, whose Emperor, **Menelik II**, had defeated a powerful invading Italian army at the famous battle of **Adwa**, the legend of the Kingdom/Empire of Ethiopia began to grow among diaspora blacks.

Indeed, diaspora blacks learnt that the Empire of Ethiopia had its roots in the powerful **Aksumite Kingdom** of the first century AD, centred on the historic city of Aksum. In its heyday, the Aksumite Kingdom was – along with Rome, Persia and China – one of the world's great powers. In the 4th century AD,

under the rule of **King Ezana**, Aksum was converted to Christianity, and ever since then has been the home of the **Ethiopian Orthodox Church**. The Aksumite Kingdom eventually fell, but was replaced by **Zagwe** and **Solomonic Dynasties** that maintained the official Christian status of the Empire right down to the reign of **Emperor Menelik II** and his successors.

The song **"Ethiopia"** was therefore drawing on an extremely rich historical tradition. It was subsequently revised by Ford, and at the UNIA's 1920 annual convention it was adopted as the National Anthem of the entire African race, and given the title of the **Universal Ethiopian Anthem!**

Menelik II

UNIA's International Convention

The Barbadian musical genius had really outdone himself and had given birth to a musical composition that would go on to become the single most important song in the entire **Black World** – an anthem that was sung wherever proud and serious black or African people gathered on our planet. The imperishable lyrics composed by Ford (and Burrell) are as follows :-

Ethiopia thou land of our fathers,
Thou land where the gods loved to be,
As storm cloud at night sudden gathers
Our armies come rushing to thee.
We must in the fight be victorious
When swords are thrust outward to glean
For us will the vict'ry be glorious
When led by the red, black and green.

CHORUS
Advance, advance to victory
Let Africa be free
Advance to meet the foe
With the might
Of the Red, the Black and the Green.

Ethiopia, the tyrant's falling,
Who smote thee upon thy knees,
And thy children are lustily calling
From over the distant seas.
Jehovah, the Great One has heard us,
Has noted our sighs and our tears,
With His spirit of Love he has stirred us
To be One through the coming years.

CHORUS – Advance, advance, etc.

O Jehovah, Thou God of ages,
Grant unto our sons that lead
The wisdom Thou gave to thy Sages
When Israel was sore in need.
Thy voice thro' the dim past has spoken,
Ethiopia shall stretch forth her hand
By thee shall all fetters be broken,
And Heav'n bless our dear fatherland

CHORUS – Advance, advance, etc.

Indeed, the Anthem was considered to be of such importance that when, in March 1921, the UNIA issued a **Universal Negro Catechism** - a question and answer course of instruction in religion and historical knowledge pertaining to the black or African race - a place of prominence was reserved for the Universal Ethiopian Anthem:

Q: Did God make any group or race of men superior to another?
A: No. He created all races equal and of one blood, to dwell on all the face of the earth.
Q: Is it true that the Ethiopian or Black group of the human family is the lowest group of all ?
A: It is a base falsehood which is taught in books written by white men. All races were created equal.
Q: Whom did the ancients call Ethiopians ?
A: All men of dark brown or black colour.
Q: What National Anthem did the Convention authorize for our race ?
A: That which begins "Ethiopia, thou land of our Fathers", composed by Burrell and Ford.

In Ford's own homeland of Barbados, this Anthem became the black Barbadian's "national" Anthem. Indeed, not only was it sung at meetings of the several branches of the UNIA that came to be established in Barbados during the 1920s, but also in organizations such as Right Excellent Charles Duncan Oneal's **Democratic League** and **Barbados Workingmen's Association**.

Hon. Marcus Garvey and officers of UNIA

One hundred years after its composition, Arnold Josiah Ford's **Universal Ethiopian Anthem** still holds the distinction of being the single most important song in the modern history of the African race!

Chapter 4

The Historic 1920 UNIA Convention

Aside from carrying out the critical function of being the primary song-writer of the Marcus Garvey Movement – composing, performing and even recording a slew of classic hymns, patriotic songs, anthems and marching songs for the various military and para-military units of the UNIA – Ford also found himself prominently situated among the several Jewish, Muslim and Christian clergymen (including the famous UNIA Chaplain General, Bishop George Alexander McGuire of **African Orthodox Church** fame) who were each trying to influence the religious direction of the powerful **UNIA**.

And so, by the year 1919, the Barbadian musical maestro had travelled far and had ascended to great heights. Not only had he made a telling contribution to the early development of African-American music, but he had also become a leading officer of what was by far the most powerful organization in the entire Black World - the **Universal Negro Improvement Association** (UNIA).

It needs to be recalled that this organization had a membership of eight million people (at its peak) organized in close to 2,000 branches in forty different countries of the World. It also possessed a variety of service and manufacturing businesses, paramilitary and non-military auxiliary organizations, educational institutions, newspapers, and a steamship company known as the **"Black Star Line"**.

Hon. Marcus Mosiah Garvey

But it was precisely at this time - in the year 1919 - when the **UNIA** loomed so large in the life of not only the Barbadian Rabbi but also of the entire black population, that Arnold Ford experienced a chance encounter that would have significant implications for the future development of his life!

The "chance encounter" that I refer to is a meeting that took place in Harlem between Rabbi Ford and the members of an Ethiopian diplomatic delegation that had been sent out to the United States of America (USA) by the then Prince Regent of the African kingdom of Ethiopia, **Ras Tafari Makonnen** - the young son of the late **Emperor Menelik II's** great general , Ras Makonnen Wolde Mikhael - the general who had led the Ethiopian army to victory over the Italians in 1896.

This meeting took place at a time when the USA was rocked by a spate of racist, anti-black riots. And it was against this background that a prominent member of the Ethiopian delegation – **Kantiba Gabru Desta**, the mayor of the city of Gondar in northern Ethiopia – not only urged upon Rabbi Ford the idea of resettling in the Orthodox Christian Kingdom of Ethiopia, but also informed him of the presence of a large population of Black Jews or Falashas in Ethiopia, and further suggested that grants of land would be made available to Ford and any settlers that he brought with him.

As we shall see, this was an idea that stayed with Rabbi Arnold Ford and germinated over a substantial period of time!

Bishop Wentworth Arthur Matthew

Indeed, it was after this 1919 meeting with the Ethiopian delegation that Ford joined forces with **Bishop Wentworth Arthur Matthew** (born in Nigeria to a Falasha father and a West Indian mother) and established the **Commandment Keepers Ethiopian Hebrew Congregation** on 123rd Street in Harlem – a "temple" that placed primary emphasis on the existence of black Jews in Ethiopia.

But let us return to the story of Ford's career as an Officer of the UNIA.

At the start of the decade of the 1920's Arnold Josiah Ford was at the heights of his powers as a musician, composer, linguist and theologian within the UNIA. A good description of Ford's importance and impact on the UNIA's activities is provided by the organization's report on the opening session of the historic **First International Convention of the Negro Peoples of the World**, which was held at Madison Square Garden in New York City in August 1920, and which was attended by 25,000 UNIA members drawn from the organization's 1,900 divisions located in some 40 countries:-

Twenty Five Thousand Delegates

This **First International Convention of the Negro Peoples of the World** was truly historic, in that – among other things - it produced a ground-breaking **Declaration of Rights of the Negro Peoples of the World** – a set of human and civil right demands and aspirations that were reflective of the type of mentality that infused men like Marcus Garvey and Arnold Ford.

Here then is a sample of the rights claimed by the 25,000 delegates:

"In order to encourage our race all over the world and to stimulate it to a higher and grander destiny, we demand and insist on the following Declaration of Rights:

1. *Be it known to all men that … the duly elected representatives of the Negro peoples of the world …. do declare all men, women and children of our blood throughout the world free citizens, and do claim them as free citizens of Africa, the Motherland of all Negroes.*

2.   *That ... in consideration of the fact that as a race we are now deprived of those things that are morally and legally ours, we believe it right that all such things should be acquired and held by whatsoever means possible.*

3.   *We declare that Negroes, wheresoever they form a community among themselves, should be given the right to elect their own representatives to represent them in legislatures, courts of law, or such institutions as may exercise control over that particular community.*

4.   *We believe that any law especially directed against the Negro to his detriment and singling him out because of his race or colour is unfair and immoral, and should not be respected.*

5.   *We deprecate the use of the term "nigger" as applied to Negroes, and demand that the word "Negro" be written with a capital "N".*

6.   *We believe in the freedom of Africa for the Negro people of the world, and by the principle of Europe for the Europeans and Asia for the Asiatics; we also demand Africa for the Africans at home and abroad.*

7.   *We strongly condemn the cupidity of those nations of the world who, by open aggression or secret schemes, have seized the territories and inexhaustible wealth of Africa, and we place on record our solemn determination to reclaim the treasures and possession of the vast continent of our forefathers.*

8.   *We demand the right of unlimited and unprejudiced education for ourselves and our posterity forever.*

9.   *That the colours, Red, Black and Green, be the colours of the Negro race.*

10. *We demand that instructions given Negro children in schools include the subject of "Negro History", to their benefit.*

11. *We demand a free and unfettered commercial intercourse with all the Negro people of the world"*

Indeed, this phenomenal 1920 **International Convention** must have been a source of great pride and satisfaction for Arnold because, not only did he and his music feature prominently in the historic event, but he also had the pleasure of hearing Marcus Garvey publicly lavish praise upon the people of Barbados, after Garvey had received the gift of a special chair from the almost exclusively all-Barbadian Brooklyn Division of the UNIA :-

"I shall continue to do for this Association my very best; and as Barbados has shown so splendidly in the getting together of the various groups – I believe they are at the head of the list financially – it seems to me that Barbados has great inspiration behind it as a country, and that that inspiration follows the citizens of that country wherever they go; and if, in sitting in that chair, I get some of the inspiration of Barbados, I shall be satisfied."

Chapter 5

At the Centre of the UNIA

So magnificently had Rabbi Ford cemented his credentials as a master composer of music at the UNIA's 1920 Convention, that by the following year – 1921 – the organization had produced a number of phonograph records featuring Ford's compositions. On one record, a soloist sang two songs written by Ford – the **Universal Ethiopian Anthem** and **Shine On Eternal Light**. In addition, the Black Star Line band recorded an instrumental version of the Universal Ethiopian Anthem.

Shine On Eternal Light is one of the great religious hymns composed by Ford, and is a composition that should really be gracing the church services of black or African churches all over the world. An extract of the lyrics is as follows:

Shine on, Eternal Light
To greet our souls this day;
Dispel the gloominess of night
And drive our doubts away.

Of all the gifts that flow
From thy great throne above,
We ask thee on our hearts bestow
The gift of Perfect Love.

Come Love, and give new birth
To man's destructive mind.
Spread where confusion reigns on earth
Goodwill to all mankind".

It is also fair to say that the Barbadian composer played a very significant role in lifting up the image of the Honourable Marcus Mosiah Garvey with compositions such as "God Bless Our President":-

Father of all creation,
Allah Omnipotent,
Supreme o'er every Nation,
God Bless our President

Guide him thro' life victorious
Save him from accident,
Grant him his aims most glorious,
God Bless our President.

It must be emphasized, however, that Ford's role in the **UNIA** was definitely not confined to the sphere of music! For example, at the **Second International Negro Convention** in August 1921, Ford introduced to the Convention a set of rules and regulations for the governance of the para-military bodies that the UNIA had established – the **Universal African Legions**, the **Black Cross Nurses**, and other auxiliary organizations.

The Universal African Legion

Ford also served on a number of special committees that were established to deal with various aspects of the work of the UNIA. For example, at the **Third International Convention of Negroes** in 1922 he was appointed by Garvey to a Committee charged with taking up the crucial matter of redeeming the stock of the UNIA's steamship company, **Black Star Line**.

It was also at this **International Convention** that Ford delivered an extensive analysis of blacks in the West Indies and in Barbados in particular. And it would be useful to include here a brief summary of the Barbadian's views, since it would give you – the reader – some sense of the internal make-up of the man:-

"He said...in the West Indies money talked, and the people were actually disfranchised because...the vote depends on the amount of property or salary earned...He instanced the trickery of the British Government in disfranchising the Negro in Barbados soon after emancipation by parcelling all the land to whites... He referred also to the fact that it was not the policy of the British government to grant autonomy to any country where the coloured people outnumbered the whites ... (and he felt this would continue)...unless something be done for the black people to establish themselves... With regards to the West Indian and American Negro, in the West Indies the Negro is always prepared to welcome the American

Negro in a brotherly manner ... He thought that the only salvation for the future of the West Indies is contact of the people with the American Negro, fraternal and commercial contact."

It should also be noted that Ford – a distinguished theologian – was always keen to address the issue of religion. Thus, at the Third International Convention, it was he who made a motion to reopen discussion on "The future Religious Faith and Belief of the Negro". After much discussion, a seven person Committee was established to study the matter further and report back to the next Convention. Significantly, Ford was selected by Marcus Garvey himself to serve on this Committee.

This provided a platform at the following year's International Convention (1924) for the Barbadian to support a proposal for the "deification of Jesus as a Black Man of Sorrows", and to also propose that such a Black Jesus be adopted as "the ideal of the Negro race" and that the UNIA's picture of the black Jesus be immediately circulated among the black people of the world.

Ford explained to this **Convention** that he "was not a Christian", but that he believed in a Supreme Being and was aware that Jesus had been depicted as a black man up until the time of the Renaissance, when Europeans substituted a European image. He also strongly urged that Blacks must produce their own literature, and said that he considered it a "disgrace" that the current generation of Blacks knew "nothing of the principles that guided their ancestors."

Indeed, he even went further and diagnosed that the Negro was suffering from "Leucomania" or "white mentality", and suggested the publication of all kinds of literature for propaganda purposes to cure the terrible disease.

We must also record that the Barbadian actively campaigned within the UNIA to replace the term "Negro" with the term "Ethiopian" as a general reference to people of African descent. This allowed the Biblical verse *"Ethiopia shall soon stretch forth her hand to God"* to be interpreted as applying to the efforts of the members of the UNIA, and it became a popular slogan of the organization.

In many respects, Ford became – second only to Garvey - the public face of the UNIA, and he was often selected to open proceedings at UNIA meetings or to represent the organization at national and international conferences.

But lest we be wrongfully led to believe that Rabbi Ford's life was all work and duty, with no place for personal matters, let us glance briefly at the Rabbi's private life.

So far as Rabbi Ford's personal life is concerned, a most significant development occurred in 1921 with the arrival in Harlem from Barbados of an attractive, bright and ambitious sixteen year old Barbadian lass by the name of **Mignon Lorraine Inniss**.

Soon after her arrival in New York City, the Barbadian teenager started attending meetings of the UNIA, and became Arnold's pupil in piano and violin. This was the start of a mentor/mentee relationship that would ultimately blossom into romantic love and marriage – but that is a detail that we will come to later on in our story! We should note in passing, however, that in as much as Arnold's marriage to **Olive Nurse** ended in divorce in 1924, it is possible that the marriage might already have been experiencing difficulties by the time Arnold first met young Mignon.

Mignon Lorraine Inniss

Chapter 6

To the Defence of Marcus Garvey

The year 1922 proved to be a tumultuous one for Arnold Josiah Ford and for every other member of the UNIA! This was the year in which the Honourable Marcus Garvey was arrested by the USA law enforcement agencies and subjected to a trumped up charge of having used the United States mail service to defraud members of the public by disseminating advertisements for the sale of stock in the **Black Star Line** corporation. Needless to say, this development threw the entire UNIA into a state of consternation.

The Arrest of Marcus Garvey

And it is now that the mettle and loyalty of the members of the UNIA was tested!

One of the first divisions of the UNIA to rally to the defence of the embattled President-General was the New York division of the organization, of which Arnold Josiah Ford was a leading member and driving force. In an **Open Letter** issued by Ford and other members of the New York division, Ford expressed his "trust and confidence in the personal honesty, integrity of character, sincerity of motive and business acumen of our President, the Hon. Marcus Garvey", and "in the name of our Ancient Race, in the name of the glorious struggle for African Redemption" appealed "to all Divisions of this Association, and to all worthy members of the Race, wheresoever, for their cooperation in this protest and declaration of confidence."

Of course, subsequent release of declassified **Federal Bureau of Investigations** (FBI) documents revealed that the **UNIA** had been illicitly penetrated by undercover FBI agents and by a number of planted "agents provocatuer" intent on destroying Marcus Garvey and the UNIA. Indeed, since Rabbi Arnold J. Ford and his small band of black Jewish followers within the UNIA were motivated by principles that were independent of Garvey's charismatic appeal, they were repeatedly approached by government agents and asked to testify against the President General of the UNIA. Needless to say, they refused to do so.

One of those undercover agents – one Andrew Battle – secretly reported to the FBI that Ford (Director of the marching band of the paramilitary **African Legion**) had stated that all divisions of the UNIA were training their men regularly and had supplied them with arms and ammunition!

In other words, even though Arnold Josiah Ford was a cultured man of the arts and religion, he also had a serious military bent and was prepared - if need be – to take up arms to defend his organization, his leader, and his people!

Furthermore, throughout Marcus Garvey's horrendous ordeal with the powerful racist government of the United States of America, Rabbi Ford remained loyal to his leader. Indeed, in 1926 – with Garvey convicted and imprisoned – and with the UNIA in turmoil, rent by faction and buffeted by members ready and willing to betray the President-General, Ford demonstrated his loyalty to and support for Garvey with a composition entitled **Potentate's Hymn** :-

God bless our Potentate
Long live our Potentate
Our chief to be.
May he our rights proclaim
In that most sacred Name
"Allah" – One God, One Aim, One Destiny

(It must be recorded, however, that in spite of his deep loyalty to Marcus Garvey and the UNIA, Ford did not hesitate to file law suits against both Garvey and the UNIA for failing to pay him royalties for the sale of recordings of his music, and in the year 1926 the Court ruled in Ford's favour!)

Rabbi Ford remained in his position as **Musical Director** of the UNIA until the year 1926. As already intimated, when factional disputes threatened to split the organization in 1925, he attempted to mediate, and continued to support his leader - the Hon. Marcus Garvey - even after Garvey had lost his appeal against conviction and was imprisoned in the United States prison system.

However, when all of his attempts to mediate and to keep the organization on track failed, the Barbadian - who had dedicated a decade of his life to the UNIA- came to the conclusion that it was better for him to leave the UNIA and to instead devote his full attention to his work as a Jewish Rabbi.

Chapter 7

A Black Jewish Pioneer

It will be recalled that from as early as 1919 Arnold Josiah Ford had collaborated with Bishop Wentworth Arthur Matthew in establishing and running the Commandment Keepers Ethiopian Hebrew Church. Well, if we are to fully understand Arnold Josiah Ford, it is important that we delve into some of the history of the black Jewish faith.

There is a long tradition in the Americas of blacks identifying themselves with the Israelites of the Old Testament. Indeed, two of the greatest slave rebellions of the United States of America revolved around the rebels taking inspiration from Old Testament texts and identifying themselves with the ancient Israelites' struggle against oppression.

Of course, I refer to Gabriel Prosser's Virginia slave conspiracy in the year 1800, and to the 1817 slave rebellion that was led by Denmark Vesey in the state of South Carolina.

It is recorded that Gabriel Prosser and his fellow conspirators strongly identified themselves with the ancient Israelites as they plotted their famous slave rebellion. Unfortunately the plot was discovered, and Prosser and twenty-five of his followers were executed.

Denmark Vesey, for his part, preached from the Old Testament, particularly the **Book of Exodus**, and taught his followers that they were the New Israelites, the "chosen people" whose enslavement God would punish with death.

And then, in the post Emancipation era there was an irruption of "Black Israelites" in the wake of the street preaching of one **William Saunders Crowdy** in the state of Kansas. Crowdy – an African American - taught that Africans were descended from the lost tribes of Israel and as such were the true Jews. This was an essential "teaching" that came to be adopted by most later Black Jewish groups.

Indeed, after Crowdy's pioneering work, other independent Black Jewish movements were founded in the United States of America, inclusive of the early 20th century **"Temple of the Gospel of the Kingdom"** in Virginia, under the leadership of **Warien Roberson**. The "Temple" practised a version of Orthodox Judaism, and Roberson's followers learned Yiddish and adopted a variety of Jewish ritual practices.

Thus, when Arnold Ford made contact with a group of Black Jews in Harlem in the second decade of the 20th century, he was connecting with a small but a deeply rooted spiritual movement.

Ford's 1919 collaboration with Wentworth Arthur Matthew in establishing the **Commandment Keepers Ethiopian Hebrew Church** is one of the key moments in the entire history of Black Judaism in the United States of America!

Though Ford was senior to Matthew and was something of a mentor to Matthew, it was Matthew who undertook the role of Chief Rabbi at the **Temple of the Commandment Keepers**, rather than Ford, the busy Garveyite and musician. The Commandment Keepers quickly developed a sizeable congregation – overwhelmingly working class in social origin – and drawn from Harlem and surrounding urban neighbourhoods.

Matthew taught his congregation that "the black man is a Jew ... because he is a direct lineal descendant of

Abraham and Solomon". Furthermore, the organization ran a **"shul"** which conducted Talmud Torah classes for children and a **"Yeshiva"** for adults. They also ran the **"Ethiopian Hebrew Rabbinical College"** with a curriculum of Hebrew, Greek, Latin and French, Sociology, Middle Eastern and African geography and history; ethics and law; etiquette, decorum and grammar.

With time the congregation would go on to support a home for black Jewish aged, a burial ground, kosher restaurants and numerous small businesses, including tailor shops, laundries, cigar and stationery stores, and an informal domestic employee referral service for the congregation of the Temple.

In June 1924, Matthew reportedly went to Germany to further his studies in theology at the **University of Berlin**, and Rabbi Ford served in his place until his return in 1927, even as Ford maintained his heavy work load with the UNIA.

The year 1924 was also the year in which Rabbi Ford took the further step of establishing his very own black Jewish congregation – initially known as **Beth B'nai Israel**, and ultimately as **Beth B'nai Abraham**.

Furthermore, subsequent to his exit from the UNIA, Rabbi Ford took yet another step forward in the year 1928 when he created a business adjunct to his congregation called the **Beth B'nai Abraham Progressive Corporation**. This corporation was reminiscent of Marcus Garvey's racial uplift business ventures, and issued shares of stock, purchased two buildings, leased apartments and operated a religious and vocational school.

But permit me to repeat here a point that I made earlier, and that should always be borne in mind if we are to arrive at a correct estimate of Arnold Josiah Ford: namely, that Ford always consciously saw himself as a black nationalist pioneer committed to building a new black community characterized by cultural integrity, economic viability and genuine black political and cultural power!

Unfortunately for Rabbi Ford, however, the year 1929 brought with it the "Great Wall Street Crash" and the beginning of the Great Depression! In these radically changed economic conditions Rabbi Ford tried his best with his business ventures, but by 1930 the writing was on the wall, and the **Beth B'nai Abraham Progressive Corporation** was declared to be bankrupt.

And so, having experienced the dual disappointments of the collapse of the Garveyite black nationalist mission and his own black Jewish effort, the Barbadian must have been filled with despair. But, at the precise time that the prospects of the black man in America began to look increasingly dim, the idea that had been planted in the Barbadian's consciousness way back in 1919 during his chance meeting with Kantiba Gabru Desta, of migration to and settlement in Ethiopia, began to gain new life and strength!

The Ethiopian government had been encouraging black people with skills and education to migrate to Ethiopia for almost a decade, and Ford knew

The mature Arnold Josiah Ford

that there were over 40,000 indigenous black Jews already in Ethiopia. These Ethiopian Jews called themselves "Beta Israel", but were commonly referred to as "Falasha".

Indeed, after yet another "chance meeting" in 1929 with the Ethiopian Falasha scholar **Professor Tamrat Emanuel** (a European-educated Falasha who was on a tour of the United States), in which the Ethiopian Jew specifically requested Ford's assistance in the uplift of the Falashas in Ethiopia, the Barbadian finally settled on the idea of migrating to Ethiopia with members of the congregations of **Beth B'nai Abraham** and the **Commandment Keepers**.

Also adding meaning and urgency to Ford's resolve to travel thousands of miles to the distant and legendary kingdom of Ethiopia was the electrifying news that had reached black people of the Americas to the effect that the coronation of **Ras Tafari Makonnen** (the Prince Regent of Ethiopia) as Emperor of Ethiopia was imminent. Indeed, word had spread that the new Emperor would be installed under the titles of *"King of Kings, Lord of Lords, Conquering Lion of the tribe of Judah"*. Could this be - many black people asked - a fulfilment of the famous biblical prophecy that ***"Ethiopia shall soon stretch out her hands unto God"***?

Ras Tafari Makonnen

Thus, when – in December 1930 – Ford set off for Ethiopia as the leader of a four person delegation comprising **Eudora Paris** (the daughter of Nancy

Paris and a singer of note among black nationalists in Harlem), a **Mr. Jackman**, a **Mr. Helliger** (who died during the long sea journey), and Ford himself, his mission was two-fold: namely, to attend celebrations of the coronation of **Ras Tafari Makonnen** as the new Emperor of Ethiopia, and to make arrangements for a site on which to establish a settlement of Diaspora blacks.

It may, however, be noted in passing that the now fifty-three year old Barbadian might well have had mixed feelings as he sailed out of New York harbor, for I have in my possession a copy of a birthday card that Ford had sent to his erstwhile student, **Mignon Lorraine Inniss**, in November 1929, in which he endearingly referred to her as "Mignonette", and on which he inscribed the following message:-

> *"The stars declare that this year is rather peculiar for thee. Governed by Saturn, an accident may happen if not careful. Be careful in the kitchen, with fire or falling articles.*
>
> *For thy 1930 program, progress is decidedly shown. An elder person thinks well of thee and will greatly advance thine interests. Be careful of strangers or talebearers."*

And, needless to say, being the master composer that he was, he also composed a song in Mignon's honour entitled "Mignonette"!

It would seem therefore that Rabbi Ford was leaving part of himself in Harlem as he set off in December 1930 to cross the ocean and to resurrect his dream of constructing a new black community characterized by cultural integrity and economic viability in "Ethiopia, the land of our fathers"!

Chapter 8

Ethiopia, Thou Land of our Fathers

Now, Rabbi Arnold Josiah Ford did not actually get to witness the coronation of the then Ras Tafari Makonnen and his transformation into Emperor Haile Selassie the First. This historic event took place on the 2nd day of November 1930, before Rabbi Ford and his delegation reached Ethiopia. Indeed, Ford and his party were only able to experience the tail-end of the historic event, but it would do us well to sketch the momentous events that took place just before the party of would-be black Jewish settlers set foot on Ethiopian soil.

The main event took place on the 2nd day of November 1930. At 7:30 A.M. on that day, **Ras Tafari Makonnen** and his wife, **Queen Menen Asfaw**, resplendent in white silken communion robes, emerged from the historic **St. George's Cathedral** in Addis Ababa behind a number of incense bearers, and entered an adjacent auditorium that had been specially built to accommodate the hundreds of dignitaries – Ethiopian and foreign – who were there to witness the coronation ceremony.

And once the Emperor-to-be was seated on the throne in the auditorium, the silence was broken by His Holiness Abuna Kyrillos, the Patriarch of the Ethiopian Orthodox Church, who proclaimed:-

The coronation is international news

"Ye princes and ministers, ye nobles and chiefs of the army, ye soldiers and people of Ethiopia and ye doctors and chiefs of the clergy, ye professors and priests, look ye upon our Emperor Haile Selassie the First, descended from the dynasty of Menelik the First, who was born of Solomon and of the Queen of Sheba, a dynasty perpetuated without interruption from that time to King Sehale Selassie and to our times".

The Emperor then gave his sacred vows, and in a ceremony lasting five hours, he was covered in gold-embroidered scarlet vestments, and was then presented with a gold sword studded with precious stones and an imperial sceptre made of gold and ivory.

With each of these presentations, an anointment of sacred oil was made to the imperial head, brow and shoulders. A magnificent crown, made of gold and diamonds, was then placed upon his head and Abuna Kyrillos proclaimed :-

"That God may make this crown a crown of sanctity and glory. That by the grace and the blessing, which we have given you, may you have an unshaken faith and a pure heart, in order that you may inherit the crown eternal. So be it."

The Empress and the Emperor

Thereafter, Addis Ababa was caught up in weeks of festivities to celebrate the historic event, and it is in these festivities that Rabbi Ford and his delegation participated upon their arrival in Ethiopia in late December 1930.

The first order of business for the master musician (and the outstanding singer, Eudora Paris) was to contribute to the coronation festivities with their own performances. Thereafter, they settled down to the business of seeking to secure a land grant that would facilitate the establishment of a settlement of their members in the fertile and rich lands near **Lake Tana**, reputed homeland of the Falashas.

In his book titled **"The Sons of Sheba's Race"**, the African-American scholar, William R. Scott, has provided us with what is perhaps the most accurate and authoritative account of Ford's early days in Ethiopia:-

> *"Unforeseen difficulties prevented the new arrivals from immediately obtaining either satisfactory work or the land grants and other concessions promised by Kantiba Gabru. These initial disappointments, in addition to the problems normally experienced by foreigners in a strange country, proved quite stressful. But, being a hardy and resourceful group, well suited to the rigours of life in a developing nation, the African-Americans made ends meet. Eudora Paris has related that for several months after their arrival she…and Rabbi Ford relied on the income derived from their work as musical entertainers at the **"De France"**, an Addis Ababa hotel frequented by the diplomatic set… Rabbi Ford, a gifted musician (also) supported himself through occasional violin recitals at the imperial court and by teaching music to the children of Warqneh Martin (an eminent Ethiopian)."*

And it was during these early days in Ethiopia that Arnold Josiah Ford – in his capacity as a master lyricist – revised the lyrics of the **Universal Ethiopian Anthem** and created a second version of the Anthem in tribute to the new Emperor of Ethiopia.

That Ford would so consciously make this link between Ethiopia/Emperor Haile Selassie and the UNIA/Hon. Marcus Garvey is by no means surprising. Indeed, Marcus Garvey himself – on learning about the coronation of Haile Selassie - wrote as follows in his newspaper, **The Blackman** :-

"The Psalmist prophesied that princes would come out of Egypt and Ethiopia would stretch forth her hands unto God. We have no doubt that the time is now come. Ethiopia is now really stretching out her hands. This great Kingdom of the East has been hidden for many centuries. But gradually she is rising to take a leading place in the world and it is for us of the Negro race to assist in every way to hold up the hand of Emperor Ras Tafari".

It should also be noted that in Marcus Garvey's homeland of Jamaica, several black working-class protestant christian clergymen, most notably **Leonard Howell**, also interpreted Haile Selassie's coronation as a fulfilment of biblical prophacy and proclaimed that the Emperor was either the second coming of **Jesus Christ** and thus **Jah** incarnate, or was a human prophet who manifested the inner dignity that was in all human beings. Thus was born the religion/spiritual movement of **Rastafari** or **Rastafarinism**.

The revised Anthem that Arnold Josiah Ford wrote in 1930 or 1931 and presented to Emperor Haile Sellasie came in subsequent years to be regarded by the members of both the **Rastafarian faith** and the **Ethiopian World Federation** (EWF) as their "National Anthem", and is – today – sung at Rastafarian and EWF gatherings all over the world!

These, then, are the lyrics – inspired by the coronation of the Emperor – that Rabbi Ford composed:-

"Aethiopia, thou land of our fathers,
Thou land where our God lov'd to be,
As the swift bee to hive sudden gathers,
Thy children all gather to thee,
With our red, gold and green floating o'er us
With our Emperor to shield us from wrong,
With our God and our future before us,
We hail thee with shout and with song.

God bless our Negus Negusti
And keep Aethiopia free,
To advance with truth and right
To advance with love and light,
With righteousness leading,
We haste to the call,
Humanity's pleading,
One God for us all.

O Eternal, Thou God of the ages,
Grant unto our sons that lead,
The wisdom Thou gave to our sages
When Israel was sore in need.
Thy voice thro' the dim past hath spoken,
"Aethiopia shall stretch forth her hand",
By Thee shall all barriers be broken
And Heav'n bless our dear Motherland.

Not surprisingly, it did not take long for Rabbi Ford – a gifted musician, an outstanding linguist, and a man of impressive personal charisma – to make an indelible impact on Ethiopian society. Indeed, he was quickly recognized as the unofficial leader of the entire African-American and West Indian community in Addis Ababa!

And when – by late 1931 – the Barbadian pioneer was finally satisfied that the promises of land grants would be honoured, he sent word to **Beth B'nai Abraham** back in Harlem to arrange passage for another group of emigrants to make their way to Ethiopia. This led to a second delegation- comprised of ten persons – joining Rabbi Ford in Ethiopia towards the end of the year 1931.

Among the new immigrants was none other than Mignon Lorraine Inniss, who, having graduated from the "Brathwaite Shorthand and Business School" in 1930, was assigned the task of working as Arnold's private secretary.

Thus, it was in the legendary, mysterious - and some might say romantic - African Kingdom of Ethiopia that this son and daughter of Barbados consummated their Pan-African love affair and joined together in holy matrimony.

But it would be wrong to assume that Mignon's primary motivation for migrating to Ethiopia was her romantic interest in Arnold. Indeed, the historical record indicates that Mignon was a dedicated Pan-Africanist who had long dreamt of repatriating to Africa. In fact, she was determined to invest her life in emigrating to Africa in order to fulfil herself as an African person and to share whatever skills she had with her continental kith and kin.

Perhaps it would be fair to say that she was just as much in love with Africa as she was in love with Arnold!

Also accompanying Mignon in that second **Beth B'nai Abraham** delegation was **Alberta Thomas** (a close family friend and supporter of Mignon), **Jane Foster, Ada** and **Augustine Bastian**, and **Thomas** and **Nancy Paris**, the parents of **Eudora Paris**. All of them had originally gone to the United States from the West Indies, principally from the Virgin Islands, and had been involved in the Garvey movement and/or Beth B'nai.

Thus, the stage had been set! It was now time for Rabbi Ford and his doughty pioneers to accomplish their historic "back-to-Africa" mission of constructing a new community in the "land of our fathers."

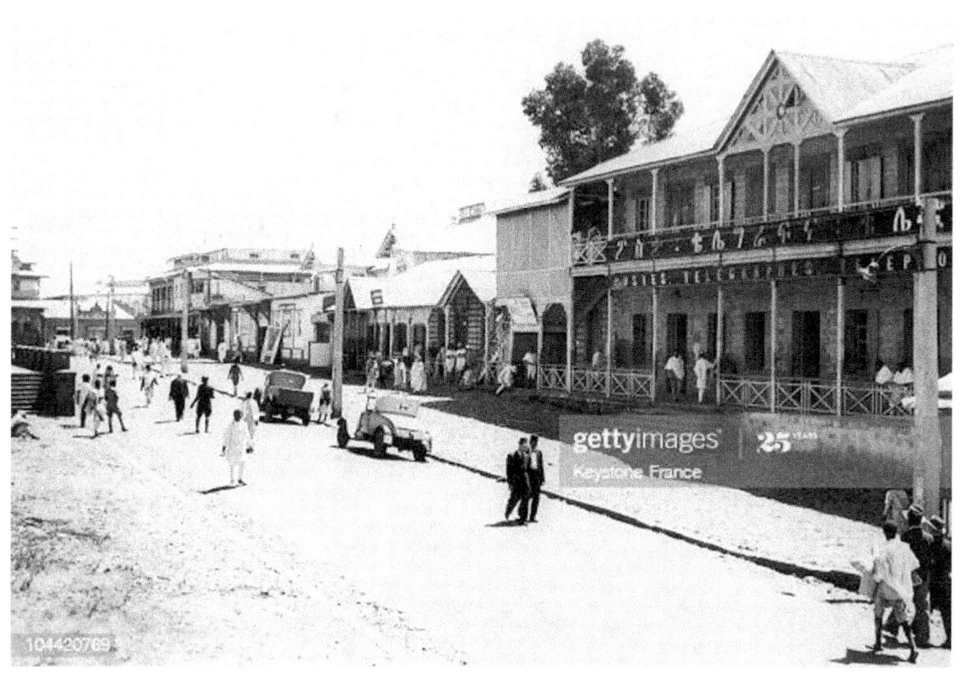

Addis Ababa in the early 1930s

Chapter 9

Striving In Ethiopia

Eventually, after some considerable effort, Rabbi Ford did manage to secure a grant of eight hundred acres of land in the **Lake Tana** region of Ethiopia on which to establish his colony. And, having done so, he was able to motivate other would-be settlers to journey from the United States of America to join his venture in Ethiopia. Indeed, it is estimated that approximately one hundred migrants came to Ethiopia to help the Barbadian develop the agricultural settlement.

Lake Tana

But, of course, as the leader of the project, the tremendous stresses and responsibilities of the massive and difficult undertaking fell on Arnold's shoulders. And, committed as he was to his vision of building a new and transcendent black community in his beloved Ethiopia, Arnold consumed himself in his sacred mission.

I cannot help but think, however, that there must have been days when the Barbadian husband and wife would have found themselves discussing the journey that had brought them all the way from their one hundred and sixty-six square mile island home in the Caribbean to this historic headquarters of the African continent, and they must have looked back with some nostalgia on Barbados. In fact, I do have in my possession a copy of an undated nostalgic poem composed by Arnold about Barbados. A short extract will suffice:-

"There is a land where thro' each tropic year
Deep-set in azure sky the sun shines clear
And balmy trade-winds from the gorgeous east
Refreshing greet each morn both man and beast.
This is my home. It's fascinating scenes,
Ripe luscious fruit and stately evergreens
Blending with white-capp'd blue of sky and sea
Sing loudly Nature's sweetest harmony"

But Arnold and Mignon would have had precious little time for nostalgia, for they found themselves fighting not only the difficulties that are to be expected when trying to carry through a massive undertaking in what was still a relatively strange land for them, but also fighting principalities and powers!

You see, unbeknownst to the Fords, the US State department constantly monitored Arnold's efforts and dispatched negative and damaging reports to Washington with such headings as **"American Negroes in Ethiopia – Inspiration Back of Their Coming Here – Rabbi Josiah A. Ford."** And, needless-to-say, agents of the American government went out of their way not only to institute discriminatory policies to curtail the travel of black US citizens to Ethiopia, but also to make things difficult for Ford and his followers in Ethiopia itself.

Clearly, the Barbadian husband and wife team was experiencing the same type of illicit destructive and subversive treatment that the racist US Government had used in the 1920s to undermine the great black nationalist movement of Marcus Garvey!

But in spite of the immense difficulties and frustrations that he faced, Rabbi Ford made it clear that he had no intention of leaving Ethiopia! In fact, he drew up a certificate of ordination (a shmecha) for Rabbi Wentworth Matthew that was sanctioned by the Ethiopian government, in the hope that this document would give Matthew the necessary credentials to continue the work that he (Ford) had begun in the United States – of directing migrants to Ethiopia.

The newly married couple also further cemented their ties to Ethiopia with the birth on 20th March 1934 of the first of their two Ethiopian-born children – the impressively named **Yosif Arnold Selassie Inniss-Ford**! No doubt, the birth of Yosif was a real blessing to Arnold and Mignon, for the baby arrived at a time when Arnold had started to experience very serious health problems.

A letter written by Arnold on 14th April 1934 to a Mr. and Mrs. Dudley Inniss of Manhattan Avenue, New York City gives some insight into the domestic affairs of the Barbadian couple:-

"Dear Dudley and Iola.

Accept my sincere Greetings for yourselves and your young and coming generation.

This letter is to acquaint you that I have been very sick, but thanks to God I am feeling fine now and instead of dying I also have got a new family and I'm trying to fight life anew.

The new wife is Mme. Mignonette Inniss-Ford, and the new arrival is a big young man.

His name is :-
Master Yosif Arnold Selassie Inniss-Ford. He is a fine big fellow. Looks like six months although he is only two weeks.

Mignon is quite well. We both send you all the best wishes, and hope that next time you will have a young man too.

I shall write you more later. Give my kind regards to all enquiring friends. May God bless and prosper you.

Yours sincerely
A Josiah Ford"

Historians and other scholars of this period have attributed the illness that Arnold wrote about in his April 1934 letter to stress, overwork, and even heartbreak stemming from the faltering of the settlement project.

Italian troops at the Walwal Oasis

And of course, one of the principal causes of the faltering of the settlement project is that by the year 1934 the fascist Italian dictator, Benito Mussolini, had declared his intention to invade and colonize Ethiopia – all in a vain effort to re-establish a modern day Roman Empire. No doubt, Mussolini - as political leader of Italy - was also still smarting from the historic defeat that **Emperor Menelik the Second** had inflicted on Italy in the First Italo-Abyssinian War at the famous battle of Adwa in 1896!

Indeed, in December 1934, while Mrs. Mignon Inniss-Ford was pregnant again and expecting her second child, the first shots in the **Second Italo-Abyssinian War** were fired, when Ethiopian and Italian military forces clashed at a fort that the Italians had illegally built at the **Walwal** oasis in a remote area of Ethiopian territory. The result of the "Wal Wal incident" was one hundred and fifty Ethiopians and two Italians dead, and this was followed by a massive build-up of Italian forces along the borders of Ethiopia.

It is in these circumstances that many, if not most, of the African-American and West Indian migrants who had journeyed to Ethiopia to be part of Rabbi Ford's settlement project began to abandon both Ethiopia and the project!

Chapter 10

Final Days and an Assessment

Sick at heart and in failing health, Arnold Josiah Ford witnessed the birth of his second son – **Abiyi** – on 5th March 1935. But this was, perhaps, the last positive and joyful experience that Rabbi Ford was to have in Ethiopia. A mere six months later – in September 1935 – we find a sick and worn out fifty-eight year old Arnold Ford extracting from Mignon the pledge that she, Yosif and Abiyi would face up to the impending Italian invasion and would forever embrace and defend Ethiopia.

And how could it have been otherwise? This - after all - was the said ardent black nationalist, who, as Musical Director of Marcus Garvey's UNIA, had composed the following lyrics for the **Marching Song** of the para-military **African Legion** :-

We are coming, oh Mother Africa,
We are coming to avenge your wrongs,
We are coming, oh yes, we are coming
We are four hundred million strong.

Every instinct in Arnold Josiah Ford's body would have told him that he had to defend Ethiopia from its enemies. And if - as the fates would have it - the tragic hand of death was to deny him the opportunity to perform that sacred duty, then surely his dear and brave wife and their sons would take up the mantle and stand courageously by the side of Ethiopia!

So, with the firm assurance of his wife resonating in his ears, Arnold Josiah Ford, that great Pan-Africanist son of Barbados, died in Ethiopia on the 16th of September 1935.

No doubt, because of the great confusion and sense of dread that had descended upon Ethiopia at the time of Rabbi Ford's tragic and untimely death, he would not have received a funeral and official state recognition befitting his status and the historic contribution that he had made , not only to Ethiopia, but to the entire black or African race.

But from our vantage point in the 21st century, it seems to me that a fair assessment of the record and contribution of this great son of Barbados is as follows:-

The life and work of Arnold Josiah Ford stands at the nexus of several important developments in black history. His musical prowess at the dawn of the Harlem Renaissance is of critical importance, and his "Universal Ethiopian Anthem" not only remains widely sung today, but may well be rated as the most important song in the world of Black Music

As a key aide and partner to Marcus Garvey, he became an important figure in the movement among African Americans to celebrate their heritage and consider returning to Africa.

In spite of the disappointments that Arnold Josiah Ford faced with his Ethiopian settlement scheme, the reality is that it was he rather than his more renowned colleague, Marcus Garvey, who had succeeded – if only briefly – in establishing a settlement of New World blacks in Africa.

Furthermore, he had done more than almost anyone else, other than Marcus Garvey, to spread the "back to Africa" gospel among the masses of Diaspora blacks in the post-World War I years.

Arnold Josiah Ford had also been one of the most important catalysts for the spread of Judaism among African-Americans, and through his successors, communities of black Jews emerged and established themselves in several American cities.

He had made an indelible and historic contribution to the development of Black Music and had been one of the most important pillars of and contributors to the glorious Marcus Garvey Movement, and to the Harlem Renaissance.

But perhaps most importantly, this illustrious son of Barbados had planted seeds in Ethiopia that would go on in the years after his death to blossom and uplift his dear "land where the Gods loved to be" in powerful ways that not even he could have foreseen or imagined!

THE
PAN-AFRICAN LOVE STORY
of
ARNOLD and MIGNON FORD
(Part 2)

MIGNON'S STORY

"Princes shall come out of Egypt and Ethiopia shall soon stretch forth her hands unto God." (Psalm 68, Verse 31)

Chapter 1

The Italian Invasion of Ethiopia

AT PRECISELY 5:00 A.M. on the 3rd of October 1935 – just two weeks after the death of Arnold Josiah Ford – a massive Italian army under the leadership of General Emilio De Bono crossed the Mareb River and advanced into northern Ethiopia from Eritrea without a declaration of war. And at the same time, a second army, under the command of General Rodolfo Graziani, invaded southern Ethiopia from Italian Somaliland.

In response to the Italian invasion, Ethiopia made a declaration of war against Italy, and thus commenced the **Second Italo-Abyssinian War**!

News of the invasion would have quickly reached Mrs Mignon Lorraine Inniss Ford at her home in Addis Ababa, and would have rudely interrupted the period of mourning she was undergoing since the tragic death of her husband.

As the armies of **De Bono** and **Graziani** began their advances towards Addis Ababa, Mignon must have reflected on the journey that had bought her all the way from the small Caribbean island of Barbados to this epicenter of international military conflict. Let us take a brief look at that journey.

Mignon Lorraine Inniss had been born on the 19th of November 1905 on the tenantry lands of **Wakefield Sugar Plantation** near Four Roads, St. John in the island of Barbados.

In her adult years, she recollected that even as a child she was imbued with a deep curiosity about her African ancestry, and had once questioned her Sunday School teacher about the absence of black children like herself from the books used in the Sunday School – inclusive of the Bible. Indeed, she had instinctively felt that there had to be something wrong or false about such books and had openly expressed this to her teacher!

Unfortunately, we know very little about Mignon's childhood days in early 20th Century colonial Barbados, but we can definitely state that, in 1921, at the age of sixteen years, Mignon migrated to Harlem in the United States of America to live with her mother's friend, **Ms. Alberta Thomas**, and to pursue secretarial and business studies.

Fortuitously, Mignon's mentor - Ms. Alberta Thomas - was a member of Marcus Garvey's **Universal Negro Improvement Association** (UNIA), and while Mignon resided in Harlem she regularly attended meetings of the UNIA where she learnt about her African heritage and gained an appreciation of her responsibility to use her skills to benefit the continent of Africa and her fellow Africans.

Mignon Lorraine Inniss

Indeed, Mignon voraciously read whatever reading material was available that showed Africa in an objective light and listened to all who had anything positive to say about Africa and Africans. She later confided that "the philosophy behind the UNIA strengthened my resolve."

Also of great significance is that Mignon became a music-lessons student of **Rabbi Arnold Josiah Ford**, and subsequently joined Ford's black Jewish congregation, **Beth B'nai Abraham**. And it is fair to say that as a result of these experiences Mignon developed a deep interest in fulfilling her destiny as an African woman by migrating to Africa and investing her skills in helping to educate her African kith and kin.

Finally, in 1931, Mignon fulfilled her deep Pan-Africanist longings when she journeyed to Ethiopia to join Rabbi Ford; to marry him; and to become the mother of his two Ethiopia-born children.

No doubt, the fate of these two vulnerable infant children must have weighed heavily on Mignon's mind as the well-equipped and heavily mechanized Italian armies initially brushed aside the much less well prepared Ethiopian army that confronted them in the first battles of the war . Indeed, the Italian armies seemed unstoppable as they captured such symbolically important Ethiopian cities and districts as **Adignat** and **Adwa** – the scene of the historic 1896 Ethiopian military triumph over Italy.

However, Mignon's hopes would have been revived when, in December 1935, Emperor Haile Selassie drew his troops together and launched what he hoped would be a decisive counter – attack, known as the **"Christmas Offensive."**

In its initial phases, the **Christmas Offensive** proved to be an outstanding Ethiopian success, with the Emperor's generals displaying good tactical skills. Not only did the Ethiopian forces succeed in encircling the Italians, but they were even able to swarm and overpower a number

Ethiopian Soldiers

of the Italian tanks. But, as was to be expected, the Ethiopian offensive was eventually stopped as a result of the superiority of the Italian forces in such modern weapons as machine guns and heavy artillery.

And then, in January 1936, the Italians started to use the "secret weapon" that ultimately guaranteed their victory in the War – poison gas!

The Italians delivered their poison gas by special artillery cannisters attached to bombers of the **Italian Royal Air Force**. And while the poorly equipped Ethiopians (many of whom only possessed spears and bows and arrows) had been able to achieve some success against the standard modern weaponry of the Italians, they had no defenses against this **_"terrible rain that burned and killed"_**.

Emperor Haile Selassie subsequently explained the decisive role that the use of poison gas played in the War as follows:-

"It was at the time when the (Ethiopian) operations for the encircling of Makale were taking place that the Italian command, fearing a rout, followed the procedure which it is now my duty to denounce to the world. Special sprayers were installed on board aircraft so that they could vaporize over vast areas of territory a fine death-dealing rain.

Groups of nine, fifteen, eighteen aircraft followed one another so that the fog issuing from them formed a continuous sheet.

It was thus that, as from the end of January 1936, soldiers, women, children, cattle, rivers, lakes and pastures were drenched continually with this deadly rain. To systematically kill all living creatures, to more surely poison waters and pastures, the Italian command made its aircraft pass over and over again. That was its chief method of warfare."

From then onwards, Mignon – from her observation point in Addis Ababa – must have experienced a gradually intensifying sense of foreboding as the Italians racked up victory after victory and systematically advanced on Ethiopia's capital city.

Of decisive importance was the March 31, 1936 **Battle of Maychew** in which the Italians defeated an Ethiopian counter offensive by the main Ethiopian army commanded by Emperor Haile Selassie himself. The outnumbered Ethiopians could not overcome the well-prepared Italian defences. Indeed, for one whole day the Ethiopians launched near non-stop attacks on the Italian defenders and their Eritrean colonial troops, but ultimately, the exhausted Ethiopians withdrew under fierce counterattack.

The Italian Air Force then finished off what was left of Haile Selassie's army by attacking the survivors at **Lake Ashangi** with mustard gas, until – on 4th April – Haile Selassie looked with despair upon the horrific sight of the thousands of dead bodies of his army ringing the poisoned lake.

Finally, on the 26th April 1936, Marshal Pietro Badoglio commenced his so-called **March of the Iron Will** towards the city of Addis Ababa. This was indeed a terrifying spectacle, and as the Italian forces drew nearer and nearer to Addis Ababa, Mignon would have seen all around her the dispiriting signs of mass fear and panic!

It became clear that the end was near when - in the early morning of 2nd May- the Emperor himself boarded a train from Addis Ababa to Djibouti, carrying with him all the golden treasure of the Ethiopian Central Bank! (It must be recorded, however, that prior to his departure, the Emperor had ordered the mayor of Addis Ababa to maintain order in the city and had appointed his son, **Ras Imru Haile Selassie**, as his Prince Regent during his absence.)

As Haile Selassie made his way out of Ethiopia, and onwards to England via Djibouti and Palestine, he explained his actions as follows:-

"We have decided to bring to an end the most unequal, most unjust, most barbarous war of our age, and have chosen the road to exile in order that our people will not be exterminated and in order to consecrate ourselves wholly and in peace to the preservation of our empire's independence…we now demand that the League of Nations should…decide not to recognize territorial extensions, or the exercise of an assumed sovereignty, resulting from the illegal recourse to armed force…."

Meanwhile, back in Addis Ababa, Mignon was a witness to the chaos that engulfed the city! Rioters took control of the streets; the city authorities abandoned their efforts to maintain law and order; and there was a deluge of looting and the setting fire to shops owned by Europeans. And then, on the 5th of March 1936, Marshal Badoglio's forces marched triumphantly into Addis Ababa and put down the unrest in the streets. The **Second Italo-Abyssinian War** was effectively over!

Chapter 2

Surviving the Fascist Occupation

Italy's 150,000 strong occupation army spread across the country, even as Marshall Pietro Badoglio - proclaimed the first Viceroy and Governor General of the new Italian colony– was replaced on 11th June by Marshall Graziani. The Italian occupation of defeated Ethiopia had begun.

Mignon Lorraine Inniss Ford now had to contend with the dire state of affairs that living in a conquered country under racist, fascist, European rule constituted! And she had to do so with two infant children on her hands, and with virtually no support structure in place other than her "godmother", Alberta Thomas. This then, was the supreme test of the solemn pledge she had made to her husband on his death-bed.

Mignon and Her Sons, Yosef and Abiyi

Almost immediately, the Italian dictator rolled out a comprehensive racist programme for the entire country, and especially for the capital city of Addis Ababa. Mussolini's first objective as commander of occupied Addis Ababa was to "de-Ethiopianize" the city, so that it could be rebuilt as a colonial capital. Thus, he ordered the removal of all the symbols of Ethiopia's historic independence, including famous statues of **Menelik II** and the **Lion of Judah**. (He also demanded the looting of the great Obelisk of **Aksum** and had many historic paintings, crowns, and other ornaments of the nobility removed and shipped to Rome.)

The Italians also introduced an explicit policy of anti-black racism and segregation. Racial intermixture and so-called miscegenation were forbidden by law, and an apartheid-type segregationist racial housing policy was imposed on the city.

And then there were the killings!

In July 1936, a few Ethiopian forces that were still intact after the war, gathered together and launched an attack on Addis Ababa. But when the attack ended in failure, numerous members of Ethiopian royalty were taken prisoner and executed by the Italians. This was just the beginning of the executions.

Indeed, throughout the period of the Italian occupation of Ethiopia there were several organized acts of military resistance by Ethiopian freedom fighters: but these acts were invariably met by reprisals, imprisonments, and executions.

By far the most extreme and brutal reprisal took place in February 1937 after a failed assassination attempt against Marshal Graziani at the Viceregal Palace

in Addis Ababa. In response, Graziani decreed a three day period in which all Italians in Addis Ababa were at liberty to "legally" execute any and every Ethiopian! This resulted in a brutal barbaric and indiscriminate orgy of killing that took the lives of some 30, 000 Ethiopians!

The young Barbadian widow and her two infant children found themselves in the midst of this horror scene, and only God knows how they survived it all!

Meanwhile, on 30th June 1936, the exiled Emperor Haile Selassie addressed world leaders assembled at the **League of Nations** in Geneva, and implored them to come to the assistance of Ethiopia. There was much drama surrounding the Emperor's appearance before the **League**. The Emperor was introduced by the President of the Assembly as "His Imperial Majesty, the Emperor of Ethiopia" , and this prompted a round of jeers and insults from a group of Italian journalists. This, in turn, led the Romanian Chairman of the Assembly, Nicolae Titulescu, to famously eject the Italians, with the terse directive -"***To the door with the savages!***"

Haile Selassie at the League of Nations

Haile Selassie then gave a stirring speech denouncing Italy's actions and criticizing the world community for standing by and doing nothing. And at the conclusion of his speech - which appeared on newsreels throughout the world - he prophetically warned that:

"It is us today. It will be you tomorrow."

But, needless to say, as stirring as Haile Selassie's speech before the **League of Nations** had been, his Resolution calling on the world body to deny recognition of the Italian conquest was defeated. In addition, he was not even granted the loan he had requested to help him finance a resistance movement. Furthermore, on 4th July 1936, the **League of Nations** actually voted to end any sanctions that had been imposed against Italy! Thus, was the last truly independent African nation sold out by the great powers of the world on the altar of naked anti-African racism!

It needs to be recorded, however, that while the "white World" callously turned its back on Ethiopia, black people from all over the world rallied to the cause of the African nation. Indeed, at the very outset of Italy's hostilities against Ethiopia, Diaspora blacks evinced a strong race-based mass support for Ethiopia through street demonstrations, mass rallies, volunteer soldier recruitment drives, medical supplies fund-raising efforts, and the formation of a variety of Ethiopian support groups.

Tens of thousands marched through the streets of major US cities and listened with rapt attention to speeches in defence of Ethiopia from the likes of WEB Du Bois and Paul Robeson. While in the Caribbean, not only did some 1,400 black Jamaicans petition the English King to permit them to enlist in the Ethiopian military, but throughout the entire region black popular anger and resentment at the racist treatment of Ethiopia played a significant catalytic role in the labour rebellions of the 1930s, inclusive of the July 26, 1937 uprising in Barbados.

In England, CLR James, Amy Ashwood Garvey (ex-wife of Marcus Garvey) and Jomo Kenyatta established the **International African Friends of Abysinnia** – an important advocacy organization – while in the USA, Dr Malaku Bayen (a nephew of Emperor Haile Selassie) established the **Ethiopian World Federation** to mobilize support for the Ethiopian cause.

Unfortunately, a combination of the high cost of travel to Ethiopia; the fact that the Ethiopian priority was for the acquisition of modern weaponry rather than for more volunteer troops; and the policies of the US State Department and the Colonial Office establishments in deterring the enlistment of Diaspora blacks in the Ethiopian military, meant that very little of this mass support culminated in actual concrete assistance to the beleaguered Ethiopians.

It was against this background therefore that the Italian occupation of Ethiopia lasted for a period of five years – from March 1936 to May 1941.

During those difficult, dangerous and desperate times, Mrs. Mignon Lorraine Inniss Ford provided for her family by working as a seamstress and as a music teacher. But these were perhaps the least of her occupation era activities!

Needless to say, this widow of the great black nationalist, Rabbi Arnold Josiah Ford, never reconciled herself to the Italian capture of the legendary African empire of Ethiopia, and sought every possible opportunity to oppose the occupation. For example, she made it a point of duty to participate in the Ethiopian resistance Movement by serving as an underground educator to many of the young Ethiopian freedom fighters who often gathered clandestinely at her home. Specifically, she provided clandestine services in English language translation and instruction in literacy to many of the freedom fighters.

Clearly, she flirted with her life time and time again, and many were the times that she suffered not only harassment at the hands of the fascist Italian security officers, but also arrests, beatings and short term detention or imprisonment!

Furthermore, during this evil and deadly period in the history of Ethiopia, the Barbadian widow was forced to bear the excruciating pain stemming from the executions of many friends and comrades – and she bore the scars of these painful losses for the rest of her life.

Yet somehow, Mignon, her two infant children, and her close friend and mentor, Alberta Thomas, were able to weather the five years of brutal racist oppression, and escape with their lives!

Chapter 3

Ethiopia's Sovereignty Restored

Now, it will be recalled that back in June 1936, Emperor Haile Selassie had predicted that the Italian aggression against Ethiopia was only the beginning of such aggression. And so said, so done!

In April of 1939, Mussolini launched an invasion of Albania, and followed this up in the following month by joining Nazi Germany in the so-called "Pact of Steel". And finally, on 10th June 1940 Italy actually entered World War II as an ally of the Axis powers of Germany and Japan, and immediately attacked British forces in Sudan, Kenya and British Somaliland.

Mussolini and Hitler

It was these developments that finally led Britain not only to launch a major East African military campaign against Italy, but to also cooperate with the Emperor and the remnants of the Ethiopian forces in an effort to dislodge the Italians from Ethiopia.

Thus, in 1940 Emperor Haile Selassie went to Khartoum in British held Sudan, where he established a close liaison with both the command centres of Britain's "East African campaign" and local resistance forces within Ethiopia.

Haile Selassie on the Battlefield

Finally, on 18th January 1941, Emperor Haile Selassie crossed the border into Ethiopia near the village of Um Iddla, and began organising the Ethiopian resistance groups. Two days later the Emperor joined Gideon Force, a small British-led African regular force, and raised the standard of the Lion of Judah once again on Ethiopian soil!

The British forces, augmented by a small force of South African and African colonial troops, as well as by Ethiopian guerrilas, launched a southern offensive from Kenya into Italian Somaliland and eastern Ethiopia, and a northern offensive from Sudan into Eritrea. In both instances, the Italians were routed and defeated.

The Emperor Re-Enters Addis Ababa

Wartime damage in Ethiopia

The Italian Govenor of Ethiopia then initiated negotiations for the surrender of the remaining Italian forces, and by May 5, 1941 Mignon, Alberta and the two children - Yosif and Abiyi - were able to breathe a sigh of relief as the Emperor and an army of Ethiopian Free Forces entered Addis Ababa. The Italian occupation of Ethiopia was all over, bar the shouting!

At the end of it all, the Ethiopian government calculated the damage to their country as follows:-

"275,000 combatants killed in action; 78,500 patriots killed during the occupation; 17,800 civilians killed by bombings; 30,000 killed in the February 1937 massacre; 35,000 killed in concentration camps; 24,000 patriots executed by Summary Courts; 300,000 persons dead as a result of privations caused by the destruction of their villages; the destruction of 2,000 churches; the loss of 525,000 houses; the slaughter and/or confiscation of six million cattle, seven million sheep and goats, and one million horses and mules."

Thus, Ethiopia had been severely damaged, and now desperately required a serious post-occupation rebuilding campaign. It is in these circumstances that Mignon Lorraine Inniss Ford stepped forward and made what turned out to be an historic and invaluable contribution to her adopted country!

Chapter 4

A Vocation to Rebuild Ethiopia

Five years of Fascist occupation had devastated Ethiopia and had destroyed the cohort of the population that possessed the levels of education and skills that were now so desperately needed if the country was to be rebuilt. In response to this crisis situation Emperor Haile Selassie launched a general reconstruction programme for the country and its people.

It was against this background, therefore, that on the 1st of December 1941 Mignon Lorraine Inniss Ford – with the help of Alberta Thomas – opened a one room elementary school in the dining-room of her home in Addis Ababa. This modest institution immediately broke new educational ground in Ethiopia, since it was the country's first ever co-educational school.

Significantly, Mignon named the school **"Bete Urael"** or **"House of Light"**- a tribute, no doubt, to her late husband, Rabbi Arnold Josiah Ford.

This determined Barbadian Pan-Africanist and educator was motivated by a very simple, but at the same time, a very fundamental idea: namely, that she was going to prepare men and women who would rebuild Ethiopia. Indeed, she declared her goal to be – "an Ethiopia that would be prepared to meet any emergency, a new Ethiopia fully capable of dealing with those who would dare to violate her sovereignty."

Mrs. Ford herself emphasized the shoestring nature of her initial effort:- "there were no desks, no capital, no textbooks and no classroom as such… one small dining room made all the room we had; six chairs and one stool made all the furniture." Since text books did not exist, Mignon and Alberta worked nights preparing lessons from the "text books in our heads"; and from some hardened lime found nearby were shaped pieces of chalk. And since there were no benches, the students made do by simply sitting on the floor.

Such were the humble beginnings of a school that would go on in the succeeding years to become arguably the most important educational institution in the history of modern Ethiopia.

The school started off with a student population of ten scholars, and since it was privately owned, it was financed solely by student fees. Therefore, in order to augment the very slender financial base of the school, Mrs. Ford quickly came up with the novel and creative idea of having the school stage and present dramatic productions to fee paying audiences.

The motto of the school was: ***"Combination of pen, book and a good character makes the ideal citizen."*** So successful were Mrs. Ford and Ms. Thomas in ensuring that their little school lived up to that motto, that in no time at all Ethiopian parents were clamouring to get their children into the school! In addition, in order to meet the tremendous demand for education, the little school organized afternoon and evening classes for some forty-five adults.

Additionally, in 1942 the School responded to a request by the ***Ethiopian Women's Association*** for help in raising funds for an orphanage. To this end, Mrs. Ford writes, produces and directs a successful play that is presented to the public, thereby making it the beginning of staged theatrical drama and comedy in Ethiopia.

Alberta Thomas

And then the fledgling school faced its first full blown crisis – in September 1942, less than a year after the school had been established, Ms. Alberta Thomas suddenly died.

Once again, the fates had struck Mignon a terrible blow. She had lost her husband, Arnold, in September 1935, and here she was, a mere seven years later, losing her other "soul-mate" – her godmother and mentor and a member of her extended Barbadian family – her beloved Alberta.

But clearly Mignon Ford was no ordinary woman! She had a Pan-Africanist mission to accomplish; she had two infant children to provide for; and she had a solemn pledge that she had given to her late husband to uphold! And so she soldiered on with her **"Bete Urael School"**, never once permitting its lofty standards to falter.

Indeed, the **Beit Urael School** continued to be a magnet for Ethiopian children from all walks of life, as well as for foreign children from the international community, leading ultimately to the school facing its second major crisis – It had become far too small for its student body!

Fortunately, however, Emperor Haile Selassie (a great believer in education) had by then become aware of this rare and very promising institution, and it was therefore no less a person than the Emperor himself who came to the rescue and made a donation of larger premises for the use of the school.

The expanded premises permitted the transformation of the school into a combination boarding and day-scholar school by January 1943. And, fortunately for Mignon, she was able to enlist the services of **Ms Jane Amelia Foster** - one of the New York-based migrants who had made the trip to Ethiopia with her in 1931. Indeed, it is fair to say that the ultimate success of this new development was significantly facilitated by bringing the extremely dutiful and resourceful Jane Foster on to the staff.

Chapter 5

The Glory Years of Mrs. Ford's School

As has already been intimated, Emperor Haile Selassie took a deep interest in the school from its inception. And by 1943 he was so impressed by the work of the school, and was so committed to continuing to assist in its development, that he requested Mrs. Ford to do him the favour of renaming the school in honour of his second daughter – **Princess Zennebe Worq** – who had died tragically on 24th March 1934 at the tender age of 16 years.

Princess Zennebe Worq

This must have been a great honour for Mignon. After all, one of the things that had motivated her late husband to make his pioneering trip to Ethiopia in 1930 was the coronation of Emperor Haile Selassie. And one of the first "duties" that Arnold Ford had performed upon landing on Ethiopian soil was to compose a musical Anthem in honour of the Emperor. Thus, there had long been a Ford family sentiment of profound respect for the Emperor and what he represented.

Mrs. Ford's school therefore became the **"Princess Zennebe Worq School"**, or simply **"PZW"**.

Now, I propose to make the bold case that the Princess Zennebe Worq School was truly a revolutionary

educational institution in the context of Ethiopia! And here then is a summary of my justifications for making such a claim:

*To begin with, the **Princess Zennebe Worq School** was centred around the notion that a healthy understanding between men and women starts back in nursery school, and that co-education was one of the principal means for fostering a responsible and enlightened citizenry. Girls and boys therefore attended the same classrooms, ate together in the same dining room, and played on the same field. The concept of a school that brought both sexes together had hitherto been unheard of in Ethiopia.*

Furthermore, in a land where only the elite could generally afford to send their children to school, Mrs. Ford established a significant scholarship programme which provided elementary and secondary education for a very large number of needy children from the working class and from diverse ethnic, regional and linguistic groups.

Then there was the curriculum of the School - the teaching of history, and a strong emphasis on the development of the students' African identities and on Ethiopia's place in Africa; the teaching of the performing Arts and music, dance and drama in particular; gymnastics; and competitive sports for both girls and boys. All of this was breaking new educational ground in Ethiopia.

I trust I have made my case!

In any event, such was the popularity of the school, that by 1945 the school population had once again outgrown the physical size of the school premises. On this occasion, it was **Her Imperial Majesty Empress Menen** who came to the rescue of PZW. The Empress graciously endowed new and larger premises, with the assistance of His Excellency Ato Amanuel Abraham, the Vice Minister of Education.

Empress Menen Asfaw

With the new premises the school was able to absorb more students and teachers, and the number of students rose to some six hundred, inclusive of some one hundred and thirty boarders. Furthermore, the number of teachers increased from the original two to sixteen, out of which eight were supplied by the Ethiopian Ministry of Education.

PZW also became famous for its annual stage productions, with most of the plays being written by Mrs. Ford herself. As a playwright she wrote (and even performed in plays) emphasizing the dignity of the various Ethiopian cultures. She also produced plays that depicted the lives of historical personalities from other parts of Africa and from the African Diaspora. Clearly, she was harking back to her "Marcus Garvey days", and would have drawn upon the knowledge and inspiration that she had derived from her late husband - the UNIA officer who had been most responsible for the many outstanding UNIA artistic extravaganzas.

But even while we revel in the successes and achievements of the school, it is important that we also have some appreciation of the many obstacles that confronted Mignon and PZW.

One of the major obstacles that the Barbadian educator had to overcome was the negative role that Euro-American ideas played in driving a wedge between Ethiopians and members of the African Diaspora. Among these was the myth that Ethiopians - despite their black skins - were not "Negroes" or "Blacks", but were instead "dark skinned Caucasians". It was also asserted, and widely believed, that Ethiopians had little affinity with and could benefit little from American or Caribbean "Negroes" (not to mention other Africans) who – it was alleged – had a moral and intellectual inferiority rooted in slavery and/or in savagery.

Of course, Mignon had long ago learnt from the UNIA's **Universal Negro Catechism** that that is *"a base falsehood which is taught in books written by white men"*, and also that there is a racial affinity that embraced *"all men of dark brown or black colour"*.

However, it was only by dint of consistent educational work, and through the exemplary example set by Mrs. Ford herself and by her "Negro" teachers, such as the outstanding Jane Amelia Foster, that Ms. Ford and PZW were able to overcome such unhealthy prejudices.

And so, the indefatigable Barbadian educator soldiered on, confronting and overcoming whatever challenges were thrown at her, and making history again and again!

Yet another example that may be cited is her April 1946 re-establishing of the **Boy Scouts** movement in Ethiopia and her simultaneous inaugurating of the **Girl Guides** of Ethiopia! Indeed, PZW's Boys Scout and Girl Guides troops therefore became Troops No 1 in Ethiopia!

The popularity of the school developed to the point where the Emperor and Empress commenced visiting on an annual basis to witness the academic progress of the students, listen to student music recitals on violin and piano, and to taste the full course meal prepared by the home economic classes. The school had indeed become the trend-setter in the nation!

And then, on 11th March 1955, tragedy struck once again! **Ms. Jane Foster-** affectionately known to her students as **Teacher Nani** - died suddenly. Yet again, the fates had dealt Mrs. Ford a devastating blow, depriving her of the last remaining soul-mate connected to her late husband's pioneering settlement efforts in Ethiopia.

Jane Amelia Foster

But as usual, Mignon rose to the challenge; soldiered on; and kept the banner of the school flying high. Indeed, it seemed that nothing could stop her! Could it be that the pledge that she had made to her husband on his death-bed way back in 1935, to always remain true and faithful to Ethiopia, is what gave her that almost super-human commitment and strength?

Whatever might have been the reason, the fact is that PZW went from strength to strength, and so impressed the Ethiopian authorities that in 1955 additional space was added to the school's facilities and the Ministry of Education rendered additional assistance by assigning and subsidizing the salaries of some teachers. Furthermore in 1963 Mrs. Ford petitioned the Ethiopian Ministry of Education and got Peace Corps teachers assigned to the School.

The School was now at its pinnacle, and in 1964, with the addition of the Peace Corps teachers, the school expanded beyond the elementary level by adding the 9th through 12th grades and becoming both an elementary and a secondary school.

In the following years, the Faculty of PZW became extremely cosmopolitan, comprising Ethiopian, Greek, Armenian, Sudanese, American, Turkish, Indian, Nigerian, Ghanaian, Jamaicans and Barbadians. And, needless to say, the School continued to perform in a stellar fashion.

Indeed, when the school celebrated its Silver (25 years) Jubilee in 1966, these were some of the tributes recorded by former students :-

"When I think of the PZW School – the school I attended as a boarder for over three years – I (think of) …the all round curriculum of the school – appreciation of music, sports, cooking, girl guide activities, academic subjects etc. – and the enlightening influence of Mrs. Ford that have helped to mould my formative years. Those childhood experiences which I then assimilated unaware are now cashing out in my life as a woman." **(Mrs. Hirut Hailu of the Ethiopian Ministry of Foreign Affairs)**

"No mention of the Princess Zennebe Worq School can be made without recalling the perseverance of Mrs Ford, the headmistress. "Teacher", as she has been called since the early days, has patiently guided the fate of the School through, at times, very difficult years. **(Yoseph Gezahegn, M. D., Haile Selassie Hospital)**

"Any mention of the Princess Zennebe Worq School evokes many childhood memories in my mind. There is of course the memory of Mrs Ford who has been a dedicated teacher and a mother to every child who went through that school. I, for one, not only acquired basic education in this school, but the many aspirations that helped me to reach manhood. For these inspirations I shall not exclude Mrs Ford's sons, Joseph Ford and Abiyi Ford, but give them a good portion of the credit." **(Balcha G. Fellows, Voice of Ethiopia)**

Certainly, the amazing accomplishments of Mrs. Ford's students was one of the genuine success stories in the history of modern education in Ethiopia. Graduates served in many leadership roles – in government, industry and commerce.

And of critical importance was Mrs. Ford's success in gaining respect for and advancing leadership and professional qualities of women in what had been a male dominant system in Ethiopia.

Many of her graduates – notably the women – went on to attend some of the best colleges in America and Europe. Some notables were – the first Ethiopian woman to serve as permanent delegate to the **United Nations** (UN); a founding member and President of the **International African Women's Association**; a concert pianist; and others who became faculty at major universities in Ethiopia, other African nations and the United States of America.

But, let us give the last word to Mignon herself. This is how she summed up her own record, and the record of the school in 1966 – the year of Barbados' independence, but also of the 25th anniversary of the **Princess Zennebe Worq School:-**

"For the past twenty-five years my life has been tied to the school which today celebrates its Silver Jubilee Anniversary. It is a great occasion for the school because it has proved to be a living institution, and it is an honour for me not only because of the fact that I have been the headmistress of the school for all these years, but also because I have been a witness to the great changes that have taken place in the country I came to over thirty-five years ago. Short steps have become long strides.

The changes wrought into the fabric of the country in all walks of human endeavour, are indeed overwhelming. It gives me satisfaction that the small school I founded 25 years ago in one small dining-room has participated in the reconstruction programmes laid down by His Imperial Majesty, Haile Selassie I. It is like a dream come true to see my former students holding important positions in various fields, and contributing something to the progress and betterment of the Ethiopian people.

With eagerness I voluntarily came to Ethiopia. When I first came I had a meaningful purpose in view – the burning desire to learn and teach in the country now my permanent home."

Chapter 6

A Pillar of Ethiopian Society

But let us now look more closely at the personal life and the personality characteristics of this pioneering Barbadian educator.

We get a massive hint about the inner life of Mignon Inniss Ford from the fact that virtually all of her students affectionately called her **Teacher Tilliqua** (Great Teacher) and **Emama** (Mother). Indeed, her personal value system was such that she never owned a motor-car, nor a telephone for that matter, and instead devoted her personal resources to adopting, raising and educating many Ethiopian children.

Her hallmark was the dignified way in which she expressed her humility and dedication. And she was held in such high esteem by all those whose lives she touched, that the home she eventually came to live in was given to her by her students and others in honour of her perseverance and dedication.

In addition, she adopted, formally and informally, and at her personal expense raised and educated more than thirty children, virtually all of whom went on to become successful contributors to Ethiopian society, inclusive of the late **Baalu Girma**, one of the most distinguished of Ethiopian writers.

There is so much more that could be said on this issue, but we will leave it there - the discerning reader can surely add in the additional details.

But, although we have focused so intently on the story of the **Princess Zennebe Worq School** and on Mignon's role as an educator, the point needs to be made that this was not her only contribution to Ethiopian society!

In addition to establishing and running her school, Mrs. Ford made multiple other contributions to Ethiopian society. A short list of these contributions is as follows:- she co-founded and served on the Board of Directors of the **Ethiopian Women's Association**; assisted in the establishment of the **Young Men's Christian Association** (YMCA); worked closely with the **Ethiopian Red Cross**; pioneered the introduction of evening adult classes; and, of course, founded the first **Girl Guide** movement and also restarted the **Boy Scout** movement that had been cut short by the war. She also served as a consultant to many women's organizations.

For more than half a century then, she was a mother, teacher, sister and friend to Ethiopians from every regional, cultural or linguistic group, and from every walk of life. **"Teacher"**, the name and title by which she was fondly addressed, was widely known and respected by Ethiopians everywhere!

It must also be recorded that during most of Mignon's life in Ethiopia she functioned as a major link between the Ethiopian people and peoples of African

Emperor Haile Selassie in Haiti

descent in the United States and the Caribbean. And in light of this, it must have been a source of great pride and happiness for her when, in the year of 1966, not only did her homeland of Barbados attain the status of an independent nation, but Emperor Haile Selassie visited Barbados and other Caribbean nations such as Trinidad and Tobago, Jamaica and Haiti.

The Emperor's visit to Barbados took place in April 1966, when the island was on the verge of gaining its Independence from Great Britain.

Barbados' Premier at the time, Errol Walton Barrow, welcomed Emperor Haile Selassie I to Barbados on April 21, 1966, and arranged for the Emperor to address the country's Parliament.

Premier Errol Barrow greets The Emperor

In his address to Parliament His Imperial Majesty stated as follows:

"I wish to take this opportunity to express my satisfaction at the fact that I have the privilege of paying a short visit to Barbados. The Ethiopian people have forever remained grateful for the contribution of the British government and people towards the liberation of Ethiopia. Fascism is an evil institution and this greater and wider cooperation was necessary to do away with it."

He then went on to note that Ethiopia would in a few days be celebrating its 25th anniversary of liberation, and added:

"The British government not only has contributed to the Independence of Ethiopia but it has granted to millions of people all over the world their independence after

adequate preparation in terms of development of administrative and development skills, and of the educational potential of the various peoples. For this the British government deserves the gratitude of all free people everywhere... I say this in connection with the fact that the people of Barbados, I understand, are going to be independent in a very short time. I say to the people, congratulations on hard-won independence. I am glad to be here with you today. I am confident that the people of Barbados are going to live up to expectations and in their independence work even harder for the prosperity and unity of their nation. May God bless Barbados. Thank You."

In his reply Premier Errol Barrow declared:

"Today we greet Your Majesty not only as the illustrious ruler of a proud and ancient people but also as the conqueror of fascism and the head of the Organisation of African Unity.......... For half a century you have been to us and to millions the world over the shining light of African Independence... The people of Barbados extend their warmest greeting and respectfully thank your Imperial Majesty for this gracious visit."

Subsequent to this historic encounter between Premier Errol Barrow and Emperor Haile Selassie, Mr. Barrow proceeded to take Barbados into Independence on 30th November 1966. And under the new title of "Prime Minister", Mr. Barrow went on to lead the independent nation of Barbados for ten unbroken years - 1966 to 1976 - and to make a tremendous contribution to the development of his people and nation. Indeed, Mr. Barrow was eventually accorded the status of **National Hero of Barbados.**

This 1966 connection between Mignon's native Barbados and her adopted homeland of Ethiopia must have been a source of great pride and joy for the Pan-Africanist educator, for when asked to describe her personal philosophy and her vision for Ethiopia and Africa, this is how she responded:-

"Our strength is in unity and mutual understanding; knowledge of ourselves through education...not for personal prestige, but for responsibility and duty to the future enhancement of our motherland and the making of a better life, not only for our own selves but for our children and our children's children. As Ethiopians, our strength lies in learning about each other, which is in itself the foundation for cooperation. The more we know about each other, the less we have to fear or hate. A good visionary idea and an open mind is stronger than any bullet."

Chapter 7

Disaster : The Overthrow of the Emperor

By the early 1970s, then, the **Princess Zennebe Worq School** had become a pillar in the educational establishment of Ethiopia – the school of choice of many members of Ethiopia's traditional aristocracy, and an institution that was patronized by the Emperor himself.

Then, in 1974, a disaster - centred around the fate of Emperor Haile Selassie - struck, not only the Princess Zennebe Worq School, but the entire nation of Ethiopia itself! And of course, we refer to the military coup that toppled Emperor Haile Selassie!

But if we are to properly understand the nature of this disaster and its far reaching effects, it is important that we get a full grasp of the significance of the Emperor and of the peculiarities of the Empire that he ruled.

In order to do so, let us avail ourselves of the writings of United Kingdom journalist and scholar, Martin Meredith, who has provided some very valuable insights on these two issues in his book entitled **"The Fate of Africa":-**

"No other African leader during the independence era was revered so widely as Emperor Haile Selassie. His defiant stand against Mussolini's brutal invasion had won him worldwide fame. Restored to his throne in the 1940s, he stood as the symbol of an independent Africa…His position as monarch of a state that traced its origins back to biblical times, that possessed a national Christian church with a tradition older than that of many European churches, as well as an ancient liturgical language and a sacred literature all served to endow him with immense prestige…In Africa he was universally regarded

84

*as an elder statesman, the host of the founding of the **Organization of African Unity** and its first Chairman. In Jamaica he was worshipped as a living God (Jah) by adherents of Rastafarianism, a religion that emerged in the 1930s and took its name from Haile Selassie's original title."*

It also needs to be said that the sheer duration of the Emperor's reign was impressive – he had ruled Ethiopia since 1916, first as Regent, and then as Emperor. Furthermore, he had wracked up impressive achievements over the years – abolishing slavery; building roads, schools, hospitals and a railway to the Red Sea; and authorizing the establishment of a national Parliament.

But unfortunately, the basic character of the Emperor's governance regime had remained unchanged. In the 1970s, Emperor Haile Selassie still governed as an autocratic monarch, dispensing titles, appointments and land in return for loyal service, and holding together his vast empire and its 27 million subjects through a vast network of personal ties.

And then there were the peculiarities and complexities of the Empire itself: the inner core of the Empire consisted of the mountains and plateaux of central Ethiopia, populated by **Amharas** (the Emperor's ethnicity) and **Tigrayans**, bound together by ancient ties of history and religion. But the outer regions had been added by conquests during Emperor Menelik II's reign at the end of the 19th century – the **Oromos** and **Somalis** – and Selassie himself had added **Eritrea** by force and coercion during the 1950s and early 60s. And, needless to say, these outer areas of the Empire were constantly in some degree of revolt.

The fundamental problem, however, had to do with the age of the Emperor. By 1972, Emperor Haile Selassie was eighty years of age – and had

already long outlived **Empress Menen** who had died in the year 1962. But with the Emperor's longevity came the problem of declining mental acuity. Indeed, some observers claimed that by the year 1973 Emperor Haile Selassie had become afflicted by senility and was therefore in no condition to govern the vast Empire of Ethiopia.

And so, when drought and famine overtook the province of **Wollo** in 1973, claiming the lives of thousands of peasants, and when – during the same year – elements within Ethiopia's military forces began to stage small scale mutinies, the Emperor either failed to respond or failed to respond effectively or decisively.

Needless to say, this emboldened those elements within the armed forces – particularly those of non-Amharic ethnicity – who wanted to get rid of the Royal Family and the imperial system.

Indeed, by June 1973, a group of radical junior officers met at the Army's Fourth Division headquarters in Addis Ababa and formed themselves into a military committee or **"Derg"** comprising one hundred and eight representatives chosen by units of the armed forces, to run the country.

Major Mengistu Haile Mariam

Furthermore, as the weeks passed, and as the **Derg** - under the leadership of **Major Mengistu Haile Mariam** – grew in confidence, it began to dismantle the whole imperial structure. For example, during July and August 1973 the **Derg** issued long lists of names of high government officials and prominent aristocrats – including Haile Selassie's closest advisers – calling on them to give themselves up or face forcible arrest. Hundreds were arrested and incarcerated in the basements of buildings in the **Grand Palace** in Addis Ababa.

The Derg then turned on the Emperor himself! In the government press, on radio and television, a barrage of attacks were unleashed. Emperor Haile Selassie was accused of squandering the country's meagre resources and of being wilfully negligent over the Wollo famine.

And then, one by one, the imperial institutions were abolished, until finally – at a four day secret meeting in September 1973 – the **Derg** voted to dethrone Emperor Haile Selassie!

The upshot was that a less than mentally aware Emperor Haile Selassie was effectively arrested, taken into military custody, and imprisoned in the Grand Palace of Addis Ababa for several months, before he died as a prisoner on 27th August 1975.

According to Major Mengistu Haile Mariam and other members of the Derg, the elderly Emperor's death was caused by "circulatory failure". But many of the Emperor's loyal followers were convinced that he had been murdered – smothered with a wet pillow.

Chapter 8

A Blow to the School : A Return to Barbados

And now, let us return to the story of Mrs. Mignon Lorraine Inniss Ford and her Princess Zennebe Worq School. Simply put, with the demise of Emperor Haile Selassie's regime came the demise of the Princess Zennebe Worq School!

On 8th October 1974 the **Derg** issued a Proclamation to the effect that all private schools were nationalized. In addition, the **Derg** – which declared itself to be a Marxist Leninist government – classified Mrs. Ford as a propagator of capitalist ideas, and unceremoniously barred her from the school's premises. Furthermore, all properties, including her personal belongings, were taken over by cadres of the military regime, and the school – renamed the **Yekatit Sidist School** – was placed under cadre administration.

Over the next seventeen years, the school was thoroughly neglected and mismanaged, and was permitted to deteriorate to the lowest possible standards, physically and academically.

During this period of time, Mrs. Ford found respite from the gradual and ongoing destruction of PZW - the visible symbol of her revolutionary nation-building work in Ethiopia - by sojourning with her two adult sons - Yosif and Abiyi - in the United States of America. Both boys, graduates of **PZW**, had gone on to distinguish themselves academically, and had both become Professors at the famous historically black **Howard University** in Washington D.C.

Then, in the year 1988 – after 67 years of absence from Barbados – Mignon Lorraine Inniss Ford finally returned to the land not only of her birth, but also of the birth of her beloved husband Arnold Josiah Ford - the island of Barbados.

When she left Barbados in 1921, the island had been a backward British colony, ruled by a racist white planter/merchant oligarchy. But much had changed in the intervening sixty-seven years, and Mignon returned to a proud predominantly black nation that had just celebrated twenty-one years of Independence.

Furthermore, under the direction of democratically elected predominantly black governing Administrations, the living standards of the masses of people had risen so high that, at one stage, Barbados attained the number 19th position on the **United Nations' Human Development Index!**

And whether Mignon was aware of it or not, the truth is that much of the inspiration that had led the Barbadian activists of the 1920s, 30s and 40s to break the oppressive rule of the racist oligarchy and to establish the foundation for black advancement had come from the said Marcus Garvey movement that her late husband had done so much to propel.

Unfortunately, Mignon's visit to her native land took place just about one year after the death of the **Right Excellent Errol Barrow** - the revered Barbadian leader who had hosted Emperor Haile Selassie's historic visit in 1966.

Mignon at Wakefield Plantation

Mignon was eighty-three years of age when she returned to Barbados after a sixty-seven year absence, and this must have been an extremely nostalgic experience for her. No doubt, over the years, she would have treasured the poetic tributes that her late husband had composed about their Barbadian homeland, and surely, her fond memories of Barbados must have been kept alive by such **Arnold J Ford** compositions as this one :-

There is a land where thro' each smiling day
Gay feather'd choirs chant their roundelay
The blackbird's carol o'er "Green Fields" pervade

Needless to say, Mignon's pilgrimage back home saw her visiting such sites as **Wakefield Plantation** in St. John, the place of her birth, as she sought to rediscover and reconnect with her biological family in Barbados.

But even as Mignon enjoyed these halcyon days in her native Barbados, events were spiralling out of control in Ethiopia!

Chapter 9

Final Days In A Restored Ethiopia

The seventeen years of military dictatorship proved to be destructive not merely to the **Princess Zennebe Worq School**, but to the nation of Ethiopia itself!

Indeed, the **Derg's** seventeen year rule of Ethiopia turned out to be a catalogue of horrors! A short list of those horrors is as follows:- Mengistu's post 1974 violent **Purge of Rivals** within the Derg itself; the 1977 – 1978 bloody consolidation of power against opposition groups known as the **Ethiopian Red Terror**; the protracted civil war against the **Eritrean People's Liberation Front** fighting for the independence of Eritrea; the 1977 -78 **Ogaden War** with Somalia; and the catastrophic **Great Ethiopian Famine** of 1983 – 85; and the list goes on.

It goes without saying that Mignon felt great pain as she witnessed the tragic conflicts in Ethiopia and Somalia and among people of African descent generally. For her, every African child that suffered or died in Ethiopia or elsewhere in the Black World constituted the death of her own flesh and blood.

She lamented – *"They are all my children and I suffer when I see those children that I carried in my arms destroy each other for reasons that are at best ephemeral, and at worst, lacking in the substance beneficial to our mutual growth and development, and ultimately, to our common heritage and brotherhood."*

On a more positive note : the Barbados-born educator continued to travel and to receive the accolades and awards that she so richly deserved. For example, in 1989 she received the **"Edward Wilmot Blyden Award"** for her sterling efforts at continuing Blyden's Pan-African tradition throughout her distinguished life's work in the field of Education. This prestigious award was conferred upon her by the USA's **African Heritage Studies Association**, and she was also subsequently elected an Elder of this organization's Board of Directors.

But, as indicated above, the situation in Ethiopia continued to deteriorate, until finally - in May 1991- as crisis after crisis unfolded, and as popular opposition mounted, Mengistu fled Ethiopia and went into exile, thereby paving the way for the country's **National Assembly** to dissolve itself and make way for a transitional government. The hated and destructive dictatorship had finally come to an end !

So, what – you may ask - was the fate of Mignon's historic school after the end of the dictatorship?

Well, it is sad to have to report that the school went through a protracted period of struggle to remain alive and to return to some level of its past glory.

After the fall of the **Derg**, the school, though in an extremely poor physical condition, was transformed into a "community school", serving the needs of the poorest of the poor in Ethiopia. In addition, former and current teachers of the school, old scholars, parents of students and school administrators came together in a valiant struggle to keep the school alive.

Subsequent to the fall of the Derg, Mignon – by now retired – recommenced living permanently in her beloved Addis Ababa, even as she enjoyed communicating with her two natural sons, a grand daughter and a grand son living in the United States of America.

But the battle to save the school and to return it to its glory days would not be a battle for the "Great Teacher": on the 15th of January 1995, Mignon Lorraine Inniss Ford died at Howard University Hospital in Washington D. C. at the age of 89 years.

The passing of Mrs. Ford was felt nationally and internationally. And in an effort to honour her, the supporters of the school successfully petitioned the educational authorities and secured permission to have the school officially renamed what so many Ethiopians had always called the school – **The Mignon Lorraine Inniss Ford School**, or simply "Mrs. Ford's School".

In accordance with Mignon's Will, her body was returned to Addis Ababa, Ethiopia where she was buried. The inscription on her tomb reads simply :-

Oh Ethiopia
To thee she was called by duty
With thee she toiled for liberty
With thine she cast her destiny
In thee she rests with dignity

What a life this "St. John girl" had lived! Indeed, what an adventure of a life!

Mignon Lorraine Inniss Ford had made an historic journey from her Barbadian native land to Ethiopia, and had embraced Ethiopia as her very own - not merely as her ancestral African homeland, but also as her "heartland". When others were fleeing Ethiopia, she committed her entire being to the defence and protection of Ethiopia, and became an Ethiopian freedom fighter and patriot par excellence.

And without a moment's hesitation, she harkened to the call of her Emperor and spent herself in the national effort to rebuild Ethiopia after the depredations and destruction of the occupation years. Indeed, she became a National Hero of Ethiopia in the field of Education and social development. Simply put, Ethiopia would not be the country that it is today, were it not for Mignon Lorraine Inniss Ford's pioneering and historic accomplishments in the field of Education and in the sphere of gender equality.

But if I were asked to find one word to sum up the life of our Mignon Lorraine Inniss Ford, the word I would choose is **"love"**. Mignon's life was not only a **labour of love**, but truly, it constituted a **love affair- a Pan African love affair!**

Oh yes, Mignon Lorraine Inniss Ford - Teacher Tilliqua - had a deep and profound *love affair:*
** with Africa and her African heritage;*

* with her native Barbados;

*with the UNIA and the philosophy of black nationalism;

* with the discipline of Education;

* with her students and with the Princess Zennebe Worq School;

* with the soul-mates who had journeyed with her to Ethiopia;

* with her Ethiopian children , biological and adopted;

* with Ethiopia and the people of Ethiopia;

*and last, but by no means least, perhaps the greatest Barbadian love affair of all time - the imperishable love affair that she shared with that great and evergreen son of Barbados, Arnold Josiah Ford.

EPILOGUE

The Mignon Ford Foundation

Abraham Abiyi Ford

In July 1998 Arnold and Mignon Ford's younger son, Abiyi, undertook primary responsibility for establishing the **Mignon Ford Foundation** in honour of the renowned Barbadian-Ethiopian educator, Mignon Lorraine Inniss Ford.

Fully aware of the paramount need to provide quality education to future world citizens, members of the Ford family, former students, friends, admirers and supporters committed themselves to the worthy endeavour of keeping Mrs. Ford's legacy alive, and continuing to fulfil her dreams.

The mission of the **Foundation** was and is to promote and carry on the legacy that this remarkable Barbadian woman left in modern education in Ethiopia, by conducting vigorous fund raising campaigns in order to improve educational opportunities for Ethiopian youth, and also by promoting mutually beneficial cultural exchanges between Ethiopia and the African Diaspora.

Mignon's son, Abiyi, whose educational path had taken him from **PZW** to **Howard University** in the USA, and eventually to a Professorship at the said **Howard University**, subsequently cemented the Ford family re-connection with Barbados with several visits to his ancestral homeland in the New World.

His most important visit took place in September 2003 when, as a guest of the Barbados Government's **Commission for Pan African Affairs**, he delivered two public lectures on his two illustrious parents and the PZW School, and also presided over a fund raising concert at the **Steel Shed** in Queens Park, Bridgetown to raise funds for the refurbishing of the PZW School.

The Barbadian artistes who performed on that memorable and historic occasion included Barbados' Cultural Ambassador, Dr. The Most Honourable Anthony "Gabby" Carter, Charles "Legend" Odell, Sing Out Barbados, Richard Layne, and Dance Strides Barbados.

The choice of the **Steel Shed** as the venue of this concert resonated with historical nuances, since this was the venue at which the great **Marcus Garvey** had addressed the Barbadian people during his only visit to the island on 18th October 1937, some sixty-six years earlier.

A special and moving treat for Abiyi was to hear a contingent from the Rastafari Community of Barbados perform the Rastafari version of the **Universal Ethiopian Anthem**.

In November of 2003, Abiyi wrote to all of the performers and informed them as follows:-

> *"On behalf of the **Mignon Lorraine Inniss Ford Foundation**, allow me to express our profound gratitude for your generosity in making a truly memorable fund raising concert at the Steel Shed possible. The generous donation of your valuable time, and the passion and warmth with which you performed on that evening has convinced us of the worthiness and timeliness of the foundation's mission.*
>
> *You have instilled in us a powerful sense of pride and a wonderful feeling of sisterhood and brotherhood that has lifted our spirits and steeled us for the challenging work ahead. It is precisely because of the love and support of people like you that we will succeed in our Mission.*
>
> *May it please you to know that you did make a difference, and that your efforts were not all in vain. In the year since you gave the concert, we have been able to accomplish a number of things. Among them, the establishment of the Barbados and the Ethiopia Branches of the Mignon Inniss Ford Foundation, and the completion of construction and dedication of a new two-storey eight-classroom building on the school grounds in Addis Ababa.*
>
> *For your generosity and for personally embracing the legacies of Arnold Josiah Ford and Mignon Inniss Ford we ask, once more, that you please accept our most sincere thanks."*

Subsequently, in December 2003, **Dr. Myrna Belgrave**, who, along with the late **Cecil Crawford** had established the Barbados branch of the Mignon Ford Foundation, visited the school in Ethiopia and initiated efforts to establish a relationship between the **Mignon Lorraine Inniss Ford School** and the **St. Winifred Secondary School** of Barbados.

Furthermore, the Barbados Government's **Commission for Pan-African Affairs**, under the leadership of **David Comissiong**, undertook to support Abiyi Ford's heroic effort to rebuild "Mrs. Ford's School" and to solidify its linkages with Barbados.

Abiyi Ford died in the year 2018, but the institution that he established - the **Mignon Ford Foundation** - and the critical work that he commenced remains very much a pressing necessity for the African people of Barbados, Ethiopia and the United States of America.